Mobil Travel Guide®

On The Road With Your Pet

Acknowledgment

We gratefully acknowledge the help of our representatives for their efficient and perceptive inspections of the lodging and dining establishments listed, the establishments' proprietors for their cooperation in showing their facilities and providing information about them, and the many users of previous editions who have taken the time to share their experiences. Mobil Travel Guide is also grateful to all the talented writers who contributed entries to this book.

Maps: ©GeoNova. This product contains proprietary property of GeoNova. Unauthorized use, including copying, of this product is expressly prohibited.
Front cover design: Julia Brabec   Interior Design: Ron Bilodeau
Front cover photo: © Getty Images, 2008
Interior images: © Getty Images, 2008; © Corbis Images, 2008; © iStock images, 2008

ISBN: 9-780841-60322-6   Manufactured in Canada.
10 9 8 7 6 5 4 3 2 1

Table of Contents

How To Use This Book

MOBIL RATED HOTELS

Travelers have different needs when it comes to accommodations. To help you pinpoint properties that meet your particular needs, Mobil Travel Guide classifies each lodging by type according to the following characteristics.

★★★★★The Mobil Five-Star hotel provides consistently superlative service in an exceptionally distinctive luxury environment, with expanded services. Attention to detail is evident throughout the hotel, resort or inn, from bed linens to staff uniforms.

★★★★The Mobil Four-Star hotel provides a luxury experience with expanded amenities in a distinctive environment. Services may include automatic turndown service, 24-hour room service and valet parking.

★★★The Mobil Three-Star hotel is well appointed, with a full-service restaurant and expanded amenities, such as a fitness center, golf course, tennis courts, 24-hour room service and optional turndown service.

★★The Mobil Two-Star hotel is considered a clean, comfortable and reliable establishment that has expanded amenities, such as a full-service restaurant on the premises.

★The Mobil One-Star lodging is a limited-service hotel, motel or inn that is considered a clean, comfortable and reliable establishment.

Recommended A Mobil-recommended property is a reliable, standout property new to our guides at press time. Look for a Mobil star-rating for these gems in the future.

For every property, we also provide pricing information. The pricing categories break down as follows:

$ = Up to $150
$$ = $151-$250
$$$ = $251-$350
$$$$ = $351 and up

All prices quoted are accurate at the time of publication, however prices cannot be guaranteed.

MOBIL RATED RESTAURANTS

All Mobil Star-rated dining establishments listed in this book have a full kitchen and most offer table service.

★★★★★The Mobil Five-Star restaurant offers one of few flawless dining experiences in the country. These establishments consistently provide their guests with exceptional food, superlative service, elegant décor and exquisite presentations of each detail surrounding a meal.

★★★★The Mobil Four-Star restaurant provides professional service, distinctive presentations and wonderful food.

★★★The Mobil Three-Star restaurant has good food, warm and skillful service and enjoyable décor.

★★The Mobil Two-Star restaurant serves fresh food in a clean setting with efficient service. Value is considered in this category, as is family friendliness.

★The Mobil One-Star restaurant provides a distinctive experience through culinary specialty, local flair or individual atmosphere.

Recommended Since by law, most fine restaurants cannot accept pets, we've included in this guide additional bistros, cafés and other more casual dining spots across the country that welcome pets to their outdoor patios.

In each section, we indicate whether the restaurant has a bar, whether a children's menu is offered and whether valet parking is available. If reservations are recommended, we note that fact in the listing. Because menu prices can fluctuate, we list a pricing category rather than specific prices. The pricing categories are defined as follows, per diner, and assume that you order an appetizer or dessert, an entrée and one drink:

$ = $15 and under
$$ = $16-$35
$$$ = $36-$85
$$$$ = $86 and up

All prices quoted are accurate at the time of publication, but prices cannot be guaranteed.

Introduction

When you go on vacation or visit family for the holidays, what do you do with your pet? For more travelers these days, the answer is to bring the pets along.

When you take your pet with you, though, your travel plans become a lot more complicated. More hotels and restaurants than ever cater to pets, but some are still cautious to put out the welcome mat. Many shops and attractions bar animals, and by law, most restaurants are not allowed to admit pets. (Outdoor cafés are an exception.)

Most important, if you don't think your pet will enjoy traveling, it's unfair to both him and you to make him come along anyway. While most pets have a remarkable ability to adapt to new situations, those who don't can get stressed out very quickly and even become ill. You want your pet to enjoy the trip as much as you do!

Before You Go

Preparation is the key to traveling successfully with your pet. That includes training your pet and getting the crate or carrier you will use for your trip. It also includes planning your route and making reservations.

Due to the fast-changing nature of the lodging industry, it is important to call ahead and confirm the pet-friendly status of lodgings before you depart. It's not uncommon for policies to change on short notice. After all, it can take just one irresponsible visitor with a pet to convince a hotel manager that pets just aren't worth the trouble.

When confirming reservations, ask a lot of questions. Be sure to double-check the fees and restrictions at each lodging. Accommodations often have restrictions on the number, size, type, or age of animals (puppies are often discouraged). Pets may be restricted to smoking rooms or certain areas of the property. Ask if you are allowed to leave your pet in the room unattended, and if so, whether the pet must be in her travel carrier or crate. Ask about whether any fees are refundable.

Try to have a confirmation mailed, faxed or e-mailed to you

before your departure. At the very least, take down the name and title of a contact person for your lodgings.

If you're traveling by air, you'll need to start very early with reservations, because most airlines restrict the number of pets they will accept on a single flight.

The safest way to fly with a pet is to have him in the cabin with you. If your pet's carrier doesn't fit under the seat in front of you or if you're traveling with more than one pet, he'll be relegated to the baggage compartment. This part of the cabin is not designed for comfort—it's heated in winter, but not cooled in summer, which is why some airlines prohibit pets during spells of hot weather.

Each airline has its own guidelines for travel. Find out what your airline's policies are before you book your trip, and let the airline know you'll be flying with a pet when you book your ticket. Reconfirm your plans 24 to 48 hours before flying, especially during peak times.

Questions to Ask When Flying With a Pet

To travel by plane, all pets need a health certificate that has been issued no more than 10 days before the flight and an airline-approved carrier. After that, the rules can get complicated. Here is a list of things to ask about when you make your plans:

★ Are there restrictions on what breeds and types of animals may fly? Many airlines have restrictions on dogs with short muzzles, like bulldogs, pugs, and Boston terriers, because their short nasal passages can cause difficulty breathing at high altitudes. Some airlines do not accept these breeds at all.

★ Are there restrictions on what times of the year animals may fly? Most airlines will not accept animals in the baggage hold if the outside temperature at every airport where the flight stops is no less than 32 degrees F and no more than 85 degrees F.

★ How much will it cost? The cost of flying your pet is determined by the individual airline and may be based on the size and weight of your animal, as well as where and how he flies (cabin, baggage or cargo). If you take your pet in the cabin, the carrier counts him as a piece of hand luggage, but you will still have to pay a fee—usually $75 to $100.

★ If a pet can't fly in the cabin, does he fly as checked baggage or cargo? Generally, to travel on your flight as checked baggage, the total weight of your pet and his carrier must not exceed 100 pounds. You can check in your pet when you check your own luggage, and he travels on the same flight with you. If the combined weight of the animal and the carrier is greater than 100 pounds, most airlines will allow the pet only to be shipped as cargo. And some airlines require that all animals be shipped as cargo.

When flying as cargo, airlines do not guarantee that your pet will be on the same flight as you. You may have to drop your pet off at a cargo terminal, and you may also have to arrange the flight through a cargo agent.

Pricing also changes: It will be based on the weight and/or the measurements of the crate. Flying cargo is one of the most hazardous ways to transport your pet. If cargo is your only option, be even more careful in planning for your pet's needs during your trip.

First Aid for Your Pet

It's important to know what is normal for you pet so that you can spot any abnormal signs or behaviors that could indicate a health problem. You should know your animal's normal vital signs, including temperature, heart rate, respiration rate and how often she eats, drinks, urinates and defecates. When you take your pet in for her pre-trip check-up your veterinarian can help you compile this list.

When is it an emergency?

The stress of travel can take its toll on your pet. Loss of appetite, diarrhea or constipation may be the result. Sometimes these problems clear up on their own as your pet settles down. Sometimes they require medical attention. If you're unsure, always be cautious and take your pet to a veterinarian. The following are true emergencies that require a trip to the nearest 24-hour emergency veterinary clinic:

Abnormal body posture
Burns
Difficulty breathing
Excessive slobbering
High fever
Inability to urinate
Ingesting poison

Jaundice
Inability to stand
Inability to put weight on a limb
Seizures
Snake bites
Uncontrolled bleeding
Vomiting blood

If your pet has been hit by a car, has been attacked by a larger animal or has suffered a serious blow or fall, take her to a veterinarian immediately, even if she seems to be okay.

Finding a Veterinarian

Finding a vet when you're on the road is not always easy. Start by asking at the place where you're staying. Pet-friendly lodgings are often run by pet lovers, and they may be able to recommend a veterinarian. Other resources include:

American Animal Hospital Assocation (AAHA)

303-986-2800, 800-252-2242; *www.healthypet.com*

This association includes thousands of veterinary care providers and offers superb tips on pet health and safety.

American Veterinary Medical Association

847-925-8070; *www.avma.org*

This association can provide veterinarian referrals from a list of more than 50,000 vets in the United States.

VetLocator.com

A comprehensive listing of more than 66,000 pet health professionals around the country.

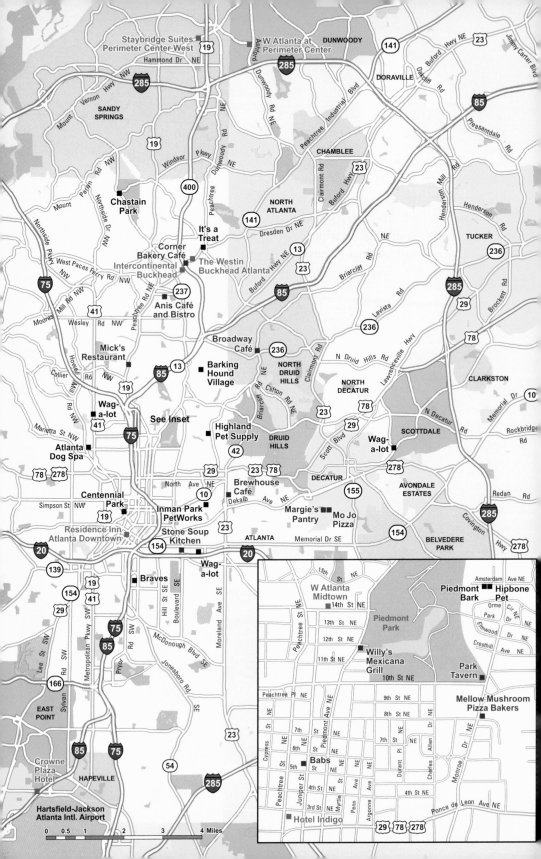

Atlanta

A short drive through any neighborhood in this Southern city unveils a not-so-disguised secret: Atlantans are rabid for their four-legged compadres. You can see it in the parks, on the sidewalks, in the sheer number of neighborhood groomers/boarders, and even the pet couture and consumer activity. Warm weather most of the year makes it easy to get outside and see the sights, or take a seat on an outdoor patio for dinner with your dog. To whittle down the options to have fun with your best friend while out in the city, read on.

Atlanta Dog Spa

707 Edgehill Ave. NW., Atlanta, *www.atlantadogspa.com*

Cage-free boarding, all-day web-cams and dog birthday parties are just three reasons why Midtown's Atlanta Dog Spa is so popular with locals. For an extra-special treat during your trip to Atlanta, sign your pooch up for a massage or neuromuscular therapy. Canines with hip dysplasia or other medical needs may also benefit from a swim therapy session. Just be sure to make an appointment in advance.

Bark at the Park

Turner Field, 755 Hank Aaron Dr., Atlanta, 404-577-9100; (season tickets, groups), 800-326-4000 (individual game tickets) *https://secure.mlb.com/atl/ticketing/bark_at_park.jsp*

The very best way to show your love for Atlanta and your love for your dog? Get tickets for one of the Bark at the Park Braves Games. This ever-more-popular event is now an Atlanta staple for dog lovers and their pups, with sell-outs each time the event is offered. A 600 dog-ticket limit per game means you'll need to plan ahead: Check the MLB Web site for more information. (Note: Sports knowledge not required, but people- and pooch-watching is a must.)

Chastain Park

Powers Ferry Rd., Atlanta, 404-733-4955; *www.classicchastain.com*

Straddling the Atlanta and Sandy Springs communities, Chastain is best known for its popular amphitheater shows during the summer months. The park also boasts plenty of activities for you and your pooch, including a network of walking trails.

Barking Hound Village

1918 Cheshire Bridge Rd., Atlanta,
404-897-3422;
www.barkinghoundvillage.com
Barking Hound Village Lofts, 568 Somerset Terrace, Atlanta,
404-875-5408; The Inn at Barking Hound Village, 2115 Liddell
Dr., Atlanta, 404-873-4960; Barking Hound Village Westside,
720 14th St., 404-870-8564; The Athletic Club, 777 Lambert
Dr., Atlanta, 404-347-9023

Urban dog owners might opt for the Village Lofts location, while the Westside locale caters to the mod dog, but whichever locale you choose, this award-winning local pet day care chain has fantastic amenities. Boarding options differ per location, but most include the choice of funky, retro motifs or quiet, serene settings.

Centennial Olympic Park

Those staying near two of Atlanta's newest (and most popular) attractions—The Georgia Aquarium and World of Coca-Cola— may opt for a Centennial Olympic Park visit. You and your leashed buddy can stroll and listen to live music some summer days or watch skaters during the gentle Georgia winters. Grab a map of the park from the visitor's center or download one at the Web site. Centennial Olympic Park was originally designed for the 1996 Olympics, and many signs of its founding purpose are seen here today, including the world's largest interactive fountain, which forms the shape of the five interlinking Olympic rings.

Highland Pet Supply

1186 N. Highland Ave., Atlanta, 404-892-5900; *www.highlandpet.com*

This Virginia Highland pet shop wins raves for its outstanding training classes and its DIY dog wash. Those with only enough time to browse the boutique's shelves can pick up wholesome pet treats, snazzy collars and more.

Inman Park Pet Works

914A Austin Ave., Atlanta, 404-522-4544

Part organic pet health shop and part art gallery, this Inman Park spot is run by Laura Saunders, an L.A. transplant (and former director of Companion Animal Services with the SPCALA). It's also one of the area's most distinctive odes to pet couture, boasting pet wear from around the world.

It's a Treat

Phipps Plaza, 3500 Peachtree Rd. NE., Atlanta, 404-846-0455;

Located in trendy Phipps Plaza in Buckhead, this shop is tops for pet couture. The $600 designer carrying bags and $800 pet beds might tempt Paris Hilton to pull out the plastic while the rest of us might stick to the less costly, but still chic, collars, bowls, litter boxes and gifts.

Piedmont Bark

501 Amsterdam Ave., Atlanta, 404-873-5400;
www.piedmontbark.com

One of our favorite events at this popular spot is the social "Yappy" Hours (call ahead or check the Web site for schedule), but the space itself, an 8,000-square-foot "indoor park" is what draws many locals. Boarding services and day care, grooming and deluxe or self-wash services are also available. And, in Atlanta's dog-loving style, it offers great birthday parties for your pet.

Piedmont Park

400 Park Drive NE, located north of the Park Drive bridge , Atlanta, 404-875-7275; *www.piedmontpark.org/do/dogpark. html*

Hot-bodied rollerbladers with small but muscular pals. Tiny poofballs in ergo-strollers. Parents and fuzzy "children" lazing

on the grass. These are just snapshots of a day in the life at Piedmont Park: the place for the city's dog savvy folks to see and be seen.

Many consider Piedmont to be Atlanta's dog lover, Shangri-La. Its diversity of visitors and range of places for you and Fido to lounge, walk, run, picnic and play make it so. The very popular off-leash area has a fenced area for large dogs, as well as a smaller run for those 30 pounds or less. This Midtown hotspot is open daily 6 a.m. to 11 p.m.

Wag-A-Lot

1456 Northside Dr., Atlanta, 404-350-7877; 225 Dekalb Industrial Way, Decatur, 404-292-3377; 840 Old Flat Shoals Rd. SE., Atlanta, 404-522-2230; *www.wagalot.com*

Atlanta's alternative weekly newspaper, *Creating Loafing*, voted Wag-A-Lot Best Doggie Day Care and we have to agree. Live web cams, photo galleries, pet massage, grooming, dog training and many different day care and boarding options make this a great place to get your pooch pampered

while you are out on the town or out for the day. For us humans, Starbucks coffee in the lobby doesn't hurt, either.

Hotel Indigo-Midtown Atlanta ★★☆☆☆

683 Peachtree St. NE., Atlanta, 404-874-9200 , 866-246-3446; *www.midtownatlantahotel.com*

During the summer months, Hotel Indigo's Canine Cocktail Hour on the patio (typically Tuesday evenings) is the place to be. Dogs enjoy free water and treats, while proceeds from their owners' drink and food sales go to the Piedmont Dog Park or Atlanta Humane Society.

Babs

814 Juniper St. NE., Atlanta, 404-541-0888; *www.babsmidtown.com*

This incredibly pet-friendly Midtown boite actually encourages diners to bring their canines to dine on the outdoor patio. Dogs are provided with water and snacks while their owners sample grilled chicken and brie panini or, during breakfast, spinach-and-goat-cheese omelets.

American menu. Breakfast, lunch, dinner; Sunday brunch.

Brewhouse Café

401 Moreland Ave. NE., Atlanta, 404-525-7799; *www.brewhousecafe.com*

Bring Spot with you to this Little Five Points fave and let him chill in the dog area or with you on the patio while you sip a Bloody Mary or taste the outstanding fish and chips.

Pub menu. Lunch, dinner, late-night; weekend brunch.

Park Tavern

500 10th St. NE, Atlanta, 404-249-0001; *tavern.parktavern.com*

This bar and restaurant is perched on a corner of Piedmont Park and welcomes dogs on the outside patio. (There's plenty of green space to run or chase Frisbees in the surrounding park.) The menu includes everything from soups and salads to superlative burgers and Southern specialties like barbecued ribs.

American, Southern menu. Dinner, late-night, lunch on weekends.

Stone Soup Kitchen

584 Woodward Ave. SE, Atlanta, 404-524-1222; *www.stonesoupkitchen.net*

This cozy restaurant has a pet-friendly outdoor patio and an ever-changing, home-cooked menu that draws good crowds. The owners also maintain a Flickr account of their customers pets.

American menu. Breakfast, lunch.

Willy's Mexicana Grill

1071 Piedmont Ave. NE., Atlanta, 404-249-9054; *www.willysmexicanagrill.com*

This Mexican restaurant has many metro locations, both inside and outside the perimeter, that serve standards like super stuffed burritos and tasty tacos. We like the pet-friendly patio at this midtown location.

Mexican menu. Lunch, dinner.

Hotel Indigo -Midtown Atlanta ★★☆☆☆

683 Peachtree St. NE., Atlanta, 404-874-9200;
www.hotelindigo.com

This Midtown Atlanta hotel is located across from the historic Fox Theater. Dating from 1920, the building features hardwood floors; original crown moldings and high, arched ceilings. After a day of sightseeing, unwind in the cozy rooms, decorated in a beachy scheme of white-washed furniture and blue hues. All pets can stay with their owners for free. The hotel's "Ruff Life" Package includes an in-room dog bed, bowl filled with treats, complimentary copy of Fido Friendly magazine, and a welcome note from the hotel's in-house mascot, Indie.

140 rooms. Restaurant, bar. High-speed Internet access. Business center. Fitness center.

InterContinental Buckhead ★★★★☆

3315 Peachtree Rd. NE., Atlanta, 404-946-9000, 800-946-7621;
www.intercontinental.com

Lenox Square, the largest shopping mall in the southeast, and the upscale Phipps Plaza are both within walking distance of this upscale hotel. Beds have fluffy white duvets and luxurious 350-count Italian linens, while baths feature showers, soaking tubs, and luxury bath products. The lovingly manicured 25,000-square-foot garden offers peaceful sitting areas and a walking path. Pets up to 25 pounds can stay with their owners for a $100 fee.

422 rooms. High-speed Internet access. Business center. Restaurant, two bars. Fitness center, spa.

Staybridge Suites ★☆☆☆☆

540 Pharr Rd., NE, Atlanta, 404-842-0800, 800-225-1237; *www.staybridge.com*

This family-friendly, all-suite hotel is located in Buckhead, about two miles from Lenox Mall and Phipps Plaza. Designed for extended stays, each suite features a full kitchen, dishwasher, pots and pans, microwave and coffee maker. A complimentary buffet breakfast is included with the rate, and there is a Manager's reception Tuesday through Thursday evenings. Up to two pets weighing less than 75 pounds can stay with their owners for a $150 non-refundable fee (for stays of over a month, the fee is $50 a week).

83 rooms, all suites. Pet accepted, some restrictions; fee. Complimentary full breakfast. High-speed, wireless Internet access. Fitness room. Indoor pool. Business center

The Westin Buckhead Atlanta ★★★☆☆

3391 Peachtree Rd. NE., Atlanta, 404-365-0065, 800-937-8461; *www.westin.com*

Located in the energetic Buckhead area and adjacent to Lenox Square Mall and Phipps Plaza, this hotel has spacious guest

rooms with Biedermeier-style furnishings and the signature Heavenly Beds. (Pups are provided with the doggie version of the bed.) The fitness center is state-of-the-art and the lap pool sparkling and inviting. Dogs up to 40 pounds are permitted; inquire about pet-friendly rooms when making reservations.

365 rooms, 11 suites. Business center. Restaurant, bar. Fitness center.

W Atlanta at Perimeter Center ★★★☆☆

111 Perimeter Center W., Atlanta, 770-396-6800, 800-916-6204; *www.whotels.com*

Located in the Perimeter Center office complex and within walking distance of numerous restaurants, shops and cinemast—this refreshing hotel offers sophistication with a modern twist. From the signature pillow-top beds and luxe linens to the contemporary guest rooms, this hotel makes for a comfortable stay. Pets receive a welcome kit with toys, treats, a W pet tag, and cleanup bags or litter box. Rooms are stocked with beds, food and water bowls, and a pet-in-residence door tag while the concierge can provide loaner leashes, toys and more.

275 rooms. Fitness center. High-speed Internet access. Business center.

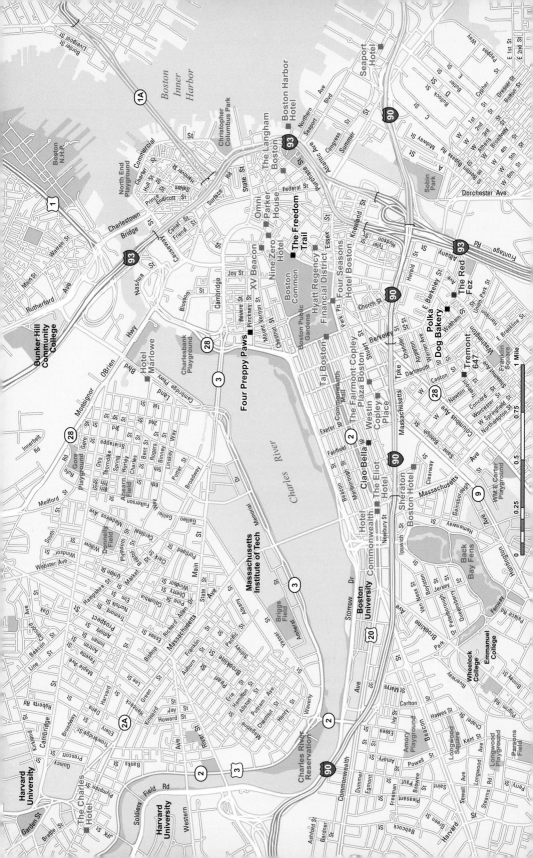

Boston's reputation as a walking city makes it the ideal spot for travelers to visit with their pets. There are activities for every season, but the spring, summer and fall bring out the best in Boston—and our four-legged friends will agree. From a morning run on the Esplanade next to the Charles River to an afternoon spent playing fetch at the (leash-free) Boston Common, there is so much to do outdoors. Many restaurants offer dog-friendly outdoor patios, and several stores invite pets inside, providing treats and water dishes for your pooch to enjoy. In addition, several boutiques and shops cater to pets, selling everything from gourmet snacks to the latest in doggy fashions.

Boston Common

Sit, Stay, See

Beacon Street, Boston; *www.cityofboston.gov*

The nation's oldest city park (established in 1634) is also a prime spot for letting dogs run off-leash, right in the heart of the city and surrounded by historic brownstones. Dogs who listen to and obey verbal commands can frolic in the park between 6 and 9 a.m. and between 4 and 8 p.m.

The Freedom Trail

Throughout Boston, *www.freedomtrail.org*

Spice up your dog's usual walk and check out the historical landmarks along Boston's Freedom Trail, a tribute to the American Revolution. The entire walk is just 2.5 miles and is clearly marked by a red-brick trail that connects 16 national historic sites. From meeting houses to churches to parks, the Freedom Trail is sure to wear out even the most energetic of pooches. Begin on Boston Common (near Tremont and Park Streets) and end at Charlestown's Bunker Hill Monument.

Four Preppy Paws

103 Charles St., Boston, 617-723-0112; *www.fourpreppypaws.com*

After a run on the nearby Esplanade, take your pet over to Charles Street in Beacon Hill for a shopping spree at Four Preppy Paws. Catering to the more upscale pooch, this boutique offers high-quality supplies and accessories for pets and their owners, including collars and leashes with matching belts for owners (in plenty of hues of preppy pink and green), bedding for pets, and much more.

The Polka Dog Bakery

256 Shawmut Ave., Boston, 617-338-5155; *www.polkadog.com*

Reward your pet for good behavior at this South End bakery. Treats are made with the finest ingredients and recipes. Accessories are also available and range from "Munchboxes" to hold your dog's treats to fashionable attire for your pet. Following that afternoon

snack, make sure to purchase one of the "After-Dinner Mints," Polka Dog's fool-proof solution to dog breath!

Ciao Bella ★★☆☆☆

240A Newbury St., Boston, 617-536-2626; *www.ciaobella.com*

The menu at this restaurant features a blend of steakhouse— robust veal chops, planks of swordfish and Italian-American specials like eggplant ravioli. When the weather is nice, diners are invited to sit outside at the sidewalk tables with their pets resting comfortably at their feet. Located on the corner of Fairfield and Newbury Streets, this restaurant offers some of the most coveted outdoor people-watching seats in town.

Italian menu. Lunch, dinner. Bar. Casual attire. Reservations recommended. Valet parking. Outdoor seating. $$$

The Red Fez ★★☆☆☆

1222 Washington St., Boston, 617-338-6060, *www.thered-fez.com*

First opened in 1940, the Red Fez celebrates the foods of the Middle East and the Mediterranean. The menu is heavy on salads and hot and cold mezze but also offers a variety of grilled meats and skewers. Pets are welcome to lounge outside on the outdoor patio at this South End establishment, while their owners enjoy their meal.

Middle Eastern menu. Dinner, late-night, Sunday brunch. Bar. Casual attire. Outdoor seating. $$

Tremont 647 and Sister Sorel ★★☆☆☆

647 Tremont St., Boston, 617-266-4600, *www.tremont647.com*

These sister restaurants include a trendy wine bar and a café that feature the full, bold flavors of chef-owner Andy Husbands. Husbands turns out the same arrestingly robust cuisine at next-door Sister Sorel café as at Tremont 647, only in smaller portions and at smaller prices. Dogs are welcome on the outdoor patio, and every Saturday afternoon, the restaurant offers treats for pets specially prepared by the Polka Dog Bakery.

American, international menu. Dinner, brunch. Bar. Casual attire. Outdoor seating. $$

Lie Down

Boston Harbor Hotel ★★★★★

70 Rowes Wharf, Boston, 617-439-7000, 800-752-7077; *www.bhh.com*

With its idyllic waterfront location and close proximity to the financial district, the Boston Harbor Hotel is a great place to stay with your pet. The hotel will provide you with maps of places to take your dog (including the nearby Boston Freedom Trail and Faneuil Hall Marketplace), as well as treats and beds for your pet. As if that wasn't enough, take your pet to the hotel's on-site spa for a treatment—even our four-legged friends deserve a chance to indulge.

230 rooms. High-speed Internet access. Three restaurants, two bars. Fitness room, fitness classes available, spa. Indoor pool, whirlpool. Airport transportation available. Business center. $$$$

Charles Hotel ★★★☆☆

1 Bennett St., Cambridge, 617-864-1200, 800-882-1818; *www.charleshotel.com*

This upscale hotel is located right next to Harvard Square and the Charles River, making for easy access to outdoor activities with your pet. The hotel welcomes pets for a $50 fee; guests must sign a pet housing agreement upon checking in.

294 rooms. High-speed, wireless Internet access. Restaurant, bar. Fitness room, fitness classes available. Indoor pool, whirlpool. Business center. $$$

Four Seasons Hotel Boston ★★★★★

200 Boylston St., Boston, 617-338-4400, 800-819-5053;
www.fourseasons.com

This refined hotel overlooks the Boston Public Garden and is a short walk to Beacon Hill, the South End, and Newbury Street. Pets are welcome at the hotel, and several amenities are offered to keep them happy. Dog beds are provided, along with dog bowls and a special menu for pets available through room service. An on-site dog-walking service is available to keep your vacationing pet in shape.

273 rooms. Pets accepted, some restrictions. High-speed Internet access. Two restaurants, two bars. Fitness room. Spa. Indoor pool, whirlpool. Airport transportation available. Business center. $$$$

Hotel Commonwealth ★★★☆☆

500 Commonwealth Ave., Boston, 617-933-5000, 866-784-4000, *www.hotelcommonwealth.com*

Close to Fenway Park and Boston University, the Hotel Commonwealth is located in Kenmore Square. This pet-friendly hotel allows two dogs (under 25 pounds) in each guest room for a fee of $25 per pet and offers dog beds and treats for your pooch to enjoy.

148 rooms. High-speed, wireless Internet access. Two restaurants, two bars. Fitness room. Business center. $$$

Hyatt Regency Boston Financial District
★★★☆☆

1 Avenue de Lafayette, Boston, 617-912-1234, 800-233-1234; *regencyboston.hyatt.com*

Located near Boston Common, this hotel is at the intersection of the financial and theater districts in downtown Boston. Pets are allowed at this hotel, but guests must sign a pet waiver upon check-in and pets cannot be left alone in rooms. A fee is charged to pet owners for accidents. The hotel offers recommendations for pet sitters.

498 rooms. High-speed, wireless Internet access. Restaurant, bar. Fitness room. Indoor pool. Business center. $$$

Nine Zero Hotel ★★★☆☆

90 Tremont St., Boston, 617-772-5800, 866-906-9090, *www.ninezero.com*

This hotel, located on the Freedom Trail, is a short walk from the financial district, Faneuil Hall Marketplace, Back Bay, and Beacon Hill. Pets are pampered here—with complimentary amenities including pet beds, bowls and treats. Pet sitters and dog walkers are available through the concierge, as well as pet grooming and pet massage.

189 rooms. High-speed, wireless Internet access. Restaurant, bar. Fitness room. Business center. $$$

Omni Parker House
★★★☆☆

60 School St., Boston,
617-227-8600, 888-444-6664;
www.omnihotels.com

Dating from 1855, the Omni Parker House is the oldest hotel in continuous operation in the United States. Its location on the Freedom Trail and close to Boston Common, Faneuil Hall and Beacon Hill make this a great spot to stay with your pet. Pets under 25 pounds are allowed at the hotel for a one-time fee of $50.

551 rooms. High-speed Internet access. Restaurant, bar. Fitness room. Business center. $$$

Seaport Hotel ★★★☆☆

1 Seaport Lane, Boston,
617-385-4000, 877-732-7678;
www.seaportboston.com

Connected to the World Trade Center, where many conferences and conventions are held, the Seaport Hotel provides an ideal waterfront location for guests visiting Boston on business. Although slightly removed from the downtown area, the hotel offers frequent shuttles to the financial district and other spots in the city for guests. The hotel is pet-friendly and allows one pet under 50 pounds per room without any additional fees. However, the hotel does require that the pet be attended to at all times.

426 rooms. High-speed Internet access. Restaurant, bar. Fitness room, fitness classes available, spa. Indoor pool. Airport transportation available. Business center. $$$

Sheraton Boston Hotel ★★★☆☆

39 Dalton St., Boston, 617-236-2000, 800-325-3535;
www.sheraton.com

Located in Boston's historic Back Bay, next to the Hynes Convention Center, this hotel offers pet owners easy access to several pet-friendly neighborhoods. Pets are welcome at the hotel and are provided with Sweet Sleeper dog beds, bowls and treats.

1,216 rooms. High-speed Internet access. Two restaurants, bar. Fitness room, fitness classes available. Indoor pool, outdoor pool, whirlpool. Business center. $$$

Taj Boston ★★★★☆

15 Arlington St., Boston, 617-536-5700, 877-482-5267,
www.tajhotels.com

This hotel, a cherished Boston landmark, has been restored to its 1920s splendor. Overlooking the Public Garden, the hotel offers a "backyard" for owners to play with their pets, plus access to shopping at pet-friendly boutiques on nearby Newbury Street. Upon arrival, a special bag with treats is presented to pets on a silver tray, and food and water bowls are also provided. Room service offers a specialized pet menu, including items such as fish, scallops, chicken, beef and biscuits, all to please the gourmet pet.

273 rooms. High-speed Internet access. Restaurant, two bars. Fitness room. Business center. $$$$

The Eliot Hotel ★★★☆☆

370 Commonwealth Ave., Boston, 617-267-1607, 800-443-5468, *www.eliothotel.com*

This 95-room European-style boutique hotel is located just off the Massachusetts Turnpike in the Back Bay area, convenient to the Hynes Convention Center and various shopping, entertainment and cultural sites. Guests will enjoy running with their pets on a well-maintained path lining Commonwealth Avenue near the hotel. Pets are welcome, but must be kept in a crate when left unattended in the room. Dog treats are provided and pet sitting is available.

95 rooms. High-speed, wireless Internet access. Restaurant, bar. Business center. $$$

The Fairmont Copley Plaza Boston ★★★☆☆

138 St. James Ave., Boston, 617-267-5300, 800-441-1414, *www.fairmont.com*

Situated in the heart of Copley Square, this landmark hotel, built in 1925, is considered by many to be the grande dame of Boston. Pets are more than welcome at this hotel, something that is emphasized by the hotel's on-site Canine Ambassador Catie Copley. The resident black Lab, Catie, happily greets guests upon arrival from her post in the lobby and is available to join guests for walks and runs throughout the city. The hotel caters to guests staying with pets and provides dog beds and food dishes upon arrival.

384 rooms. High-speed Internet access. Restaurant, bar. Fitness room. Business center. $$$

The Langham Boston ★★★☆☆

250 Franklin St., Boston, 617-451-1900, 800-791-7781;
boston.langhamhotels.com

Located in the heart of the financial district, the Langham Hotel is close to nearby Faneuil Hall, the Freedom Trail and several other historical sites. Pets are accepted for a fee of $50; you must sign a waiver, and four-legged friends must be crated when unattended.

325 rooms. High-speed Internet access. Restaurant, bar. Fitness room, spa. Indoor pool, whirlpool. Airport transportation available. Business center. $$$

Westin Copley Place ★★★☆☆

10 Huntington Ave., Boston, 617-262-9600, 800-937-8461;
www.starwoodhotels.com/westin/copleyplace

This hotel, located in Copley Square, is connected to the Copley Place Mall. Guests traveling with pets will appreciate the Heavenly Doggy beds that are available, as well as the water dishes and scented doggy bags for post walk dips. Visit the concierge desk for a full list of pet sitters and dog walkers in the area. Pets must weigh 40 pounds or less.

803 rooms. High-speed Internet access. Three restaurants, three bars. Fitness room, spa. Indoor pool, whirlpool. Airport transportation available. Business center. $$$

XV Beacon ★★★★☆

15 Beacon St., Boston, 617-670-1500, 877-982-3226;
www.xvbeacon.com

This turn-of-the-century Beaux Arts building in Beacon Hill is a highly stylized and seductive place to stay. In this location close to Boston Common and the Public Garden, not to mention the Freedom Trail, guests can easily find plenty of space to spend time outdoors with their pet. Guests are required to sign a pet waiver and pets staying at the hotel must weigh less than 20 pounds.

63 rooms. High-speed Internet access. Restaurant, bar. Fitness room. Whirlpool. Airport transportation available. $$$$

Hotel Marlowe ★★★☆☆

25 Edwin H. Land Blvd., Cambridge, 617-868-8000, 800-825-7140; *www.hotelmarlowe.com*

The Hotel Marlowe, on the other side of the Charles River from Boston, is close to a shopping mall and the Museum of Science. It's rare to find a hotel that caters to pets as much as the Marlowe does. Sign up at least 72 hours in advance for a "Pampered Pet Package" ($75), with its specially designed amenities for cats and dogs. The "Man's Best Friend Pampering Kit" includes a cozy bed, fleece blanket and lunch box full of gourmet treats from the Polka Dog Bakery, while the "Finicky Feline Pampering Kit" offers the same, in addition to a scratching post. Pets that stay at the hotel five times become members of the VIP (Very Important Pet) program.

236 rooms. High-speed, wireless Internet access. Restaurant, bar. Fitness room. Airport transportation available. Business center. $$$

Chicago

S ome may call Chicago the Second City, but thousands of pet owners say it is second to none. Part of Chicago's dog-friendliness has to do with its location and weather. Long winters mean people are anxious to get out on the first nice day of the year, and they want to take their dogs with them. Lakefront parks and beaches, outdoor cafés, and funky boutiques with all manner of treats for humans and pets are scattered along the streets of this very walkable city.

Scarcely a neighborhood in Chicago doesn't offer something for dogs and their owners. When in doubt, head toward Lake Michigan, particularly on the North Side and downtown.

Chicago White Sox Dog Day

Sit, Stay, See

US Cellular Field, 333 W. 35th St., Chicago, 312-674-1000; *chicago.whitesox.mlb.com*

What could be better than a baseball game on a summer's day? A baseball game with your dog. For that reason, the one or two Dog Days a year, held in May or September, always sell out early. Dog owners can bring their pups for an on-field pet parade, pet massages and a special sod rest area.

Mercury Cruiseline's Canine Cruise

N. Michigan Ave. and E. Wacker Dr., Chicago, 312-332-1353; *www.mercuryskylinecruiseline.com*

Grab your leash and head to Navy Pier to board one of these dog-friendly tours of Lake Michigan. Seaworthy pups enjoy the 90-minute Canine Cruises, which typically dock every Sunday until the end of summer or the weather turns chilly, whichever comes first. Reservations are not accepted, so arrive early.

Montrose Dog Beach

4600 N. Lake Shore Dr., Chicago; *www.mondog.org*

This Chicago Park District dog beach is the only legal place for dogs to swim in Lake Michigan in the city of Chicago. While folks refer to this as "Montrose Beach," it's located at Wilson Avenue, north of Montrose Harbor.

The fenced-in area provides room for dogs to run and swim, and there's typically plenty of parking during the week (weekends can be trickier, particularly when there's an event in the lakeside park).

At all of the Chicago Park District dog-friendly parks, dogs must have a $5 permit to enter the park. Permits must be issued by a Chicago-area veterinarian; a list of participating veterinarians is available at *www.chicagoparkdistrict.com*.

If taking a sandy dog back to the hotel after a day at the beach is not your idea of a good time, stop for a DIY bath at nearby Soggy Paws. (1148 W. Leland Ave., Chicago, 773-334-7663; *www.soggypaws.com*)

Chow time

Dine

733 W. Madison St., 312-602-2100; *www.ichotelsgroup.com*

Connected to the new Crowne Plaza Chicago Metro Hotel, this 1940's-style martini bar serves classic American comfort food with a retro vibe. The outdoor tables welcome dogs, and on request, they'll be served water and treats.

American menu. Breakfast, lunch, dinner. Bar. Outdoor seating. $$

Dunlay's on the Square

3137 W. Logan Blvd., Chicago, 773-227-2400; *www.dunlaysonthesquare.com*.

Related to Lincoln Park's Dunlay's on Clark, this Logan Square neighborhood grill is known for its enormous cookie skillet dessert. Other yummy edibles are the oatmeal pancakes and breakfast potatoes. Dunlay's also has a large patio with ample outdoor seating, meaning there is plenty of room for dogs. Not only are they welcome, Dunlay's makes its own smoked pig ear for canine customers, which is as popular as the cookie is with humans.

American menu. Casual attire. Outdoor seating. $$

Scoozi ★★☆☆☆

410 W. Huron St., Chicago, 312-943-5900; *www.leye.com*

An early pioneer of now-booming River North, this Italian concept—once hip, now comfortable—is a convivial place to gather for cracker-crust pizzas, goodies from the generous antipasto bar, or full-blown Italian dining. Mondays in warm weather feature "Doggie Dining" on the outdoor patio. A pet menu includes options like K-9 Cannoli, Muttini, Puppy Pizza, and Bow Wow Burger and Polenta Fries.

Italian menu. Dinner. Bar. Children's menu. Business casual attire. Reservations recommended. Valet parking. Outdoor seating. $$

Wishbone ★☆☆☆☆

1001 W. Washington Blvd., Chicago, 312-850-2663; *www.wishbonechicago.com*

Casual Southern dishes at reasonable prices in colorful settings filled with faux-outdoor art comprise the winning combination at Wishbone. Lunches and dinners include bean-based hoppin' John, blackened catfish, and shrimp and grits. Breakfast offers plenty of unusual choices, such as crab cakes, to round out the egg offerings. Well-behaved dogs are welcome at the outdoor dining area.

American menu. Breakfast, lunch, dinner, brunch. Bar. Children's menu. Casual attire. Reservations recommended. Valet parking. Outdoor seating. $$

Lie Down

The Fairmont Chicago ★★★☆☆

200 N. Columbus Dr., Chicago, 312-565-8000, 800-257-7544; *www.fairmont.com/Chicago/*

The Fairmont hotel is at once traditional and contemporary. Just a short distance from the lake and near the renowned shopping of the Magnificent Mile, its sleek tower rests on the edge of leafy Grant and Millennium parks. The interiors are refined, with rich colors and antique reproductions, and spectacular lakefront views define many of the elegant accommodations. The comprehensive business center keeps travelers in touch with the office, while fitness-minded visitors appreciate the guest privileges at the adjoining Lakeshore Athletic Club and Waves day spa. Noteworthy for its indoor rock-climbing wall, this establishment is often considered the city's top exercise facility. Pets weighing less than 20 pounds are welcome to stay here. Dogs must be crated when left alone in the room.

687 rooms. High-speed Internet access. Restaurant, bar. Fitness room, fitness classes available. Indoor pool, outdoor pool, whirlpool. Airport transportation available. Business center. $$

Hotel Monaco Chicago ★★★☆☆

225 N. Wabash Ave., Chicago, 312-960-8500, 866-610-0081; *www.monaco-chicago.com*

In the heart of downtown, between the Loop and the Magnificent Mile, the Monaco's funky, Euro aesthetic is equally suited to business or pleasure travel. The lobby has the feel of a posh living room, with a grand limestone fireplace. Colorful rooms are retreats with creature comforts, including plush furnishings and distinctive bath products. Enjoy round-the-clock room service or visit the destination-worthy South Water Kitchen, the hotel's restaurant, for breakfast, lunch or dinner. Like other hotels owned by the Kimpton boutique hotel chain, the Monaco is exceedingly pet-friendly. Check in at the front desk (which looks like a vintage steamer trunk) and your pooch will be greeted by name. The PAWS (Pets Are Worth Saving) Chicago Pet Package includes a deluxe room for both of you on the pet floor; a bowl, a bed (for dogs) or litter box (for

cats), and a treat; a leash; and a book on pet massage. Staff can arrange pet-sitting and walking services and spa treatments. The Monaco is a short walk from the Chicago River, perfect for a leisurely leashed stroll.

192 rooms. High-speed, wireless Internet access. Restaurant, bar. Fitness room. Airport transportation available. Business center. $$

Palmer House Hilton ★★★☆☆

17 E. Monroe St., Chicago, 312-726-7500 ; 800-445-8667; *www.hilton.com*

Grand and gilded, the Palmer House Hilton has harbored visitors to the Windy City for 130 years, making it America's longest-operating hotel. This Loop landmark has undergone a full renovation to restore designer-builder Potter Palmer's original French Empire opulence, including the breathtaking Beaux Arts ceiling in the palatial lobby. Amenities include an 11-room penthouse suite, executive levels with a private elevator, an entire floor of deluxe-tech conference and meeting facilities, a fitness club, and a shopping arcade. Pets up to 85 pounds are welcomed, although owners are asked to sign a waiver stating that they're responsible for any pet-related damage. In the historic

Urban Legends

Animals play a big part in some of Chicago's most famous lore. The Great Chicago Fire of 1871 was for years attributed to a cow that allegedly kicked over a lit lantern in Irish immigrant Catherine O'Leary's barn. Though Mrs. O'Leary and her cow have since been exonerated of sparking the fire, which destroyed much of downtown Chicago, the legend lives on in song and folklore.

Equally famous is the Curse of the Billy Goat, the nation's longest standing baseball curse. Legend has it that a local tavern owner, who brought his pet goat to Wrigley Field in 1945 but was kicked out of the baseball game because of the animal's odor, placed a curse on the Cubs, which have not won a championship since 1908.

elevator, small dogs should be carried in owners' arms. Large dogs are asked to take the service elevator, but that shouldn't be interpreted as a snooty attitude toward pups. The staff couldn't be dog-friendlier.

1,639 rooms. High-speed Internet access. Two restaurants, two bars. Fitness room. Indoor pool, whirlpool. Airport transportation available. Business center. $$

The Peninsula Chicago ★★★★★

108 E. Superior St., Chicago, 312-337-2888, 866-288-8889; *chicago.peninsula.com*

Reigning over Chicago's famed Magnificent Mile, the Peninsula Chicago hotel has a sun-filled lobby and gleaming, gilded details. With Tiffany and Ralph Lauren downstairs and Saks and Neiman Marcus across the street, the bellmen outfitted in crisp white uniforms are a shopper's savior. Asian sensibilities are expertly blended with details highlighting the city's Art Deco heritage in the public spaces. Soft lighting, polished woods, and golden hues make the guest rooms sparkle. Proving the point that modern amenities are a hallmark of this property, all rooms are fitted with bedside electronic control panels and flat-screen televisions. Dogs under 20 pounds at the Peninsula are pampered as much as their masters. With special beds, their own room service menus, and $85 doggie massages, the hotel takes the comfort of small four-legged friends seriously.

339 rooms. High-speed, wireless Internet access. Four restaurants, bar. Fitness room, fitness classes available, spa. Indoor pool, whirlpool. Airport transportation available. Business center. $$$$

Sofitel Chicago Water Tower ★★★☆☆

20 E. Chestnut St., Chicago, 312-324-4000, 800-763-4835; *www.sofitel.com*

A stunning design created by French architect Jean-Paul Viguier gives this hotel an unmistakable presence on the Gold Coast, just off the Magnificent Mile. Guest rooms feature unobstructed views, wicker baskets with amenities, and Roger Gallet bath products. Le Bar is a popular after-work place to meet and mingle, while Café des Architectes serves up French cuisine in a contemporary setting. During warm months, dogs can join their owners here to dine outside, and order from a special pet menu. Very much in French-style, it is smaller dogs—25 pounds or under—who are welcome to stay here. Dogs of all sizes come for the annual pet Halloween costume contest.

415 rooms. High-speed, wireless Internet access. Restaurant, bar. Fitness room. Airport transportation available. Business center. $$$

The Ritz-Carlton, A Four Seasons Hotel

★★★★★

160 E. Pearson St., Chicago, 312-266-1000, 800-621-6906;
www.fourseasons.com/chicagorc/

The unparalleled levels of service, commitment to excellence, and meticulous attention to detail make this hotel one of the country's finest. Located on the upper levels of Water Tower Place on the Magnificent Mile, the hotel's guest rooms afford picture-perfect views through large windows. Managed by the Four Seasons, the Ritz-Carlton offers guests a taste of the luxe life, from the decor and seamless service to the superlative cuisine at its restaurants and lounges. Human guests, however, are not the only ones to be spoiled: Furry visitors (under 30 pounds) feast in-room on filet mignon and salmon. Dogs may not be left unattended, but pet-sitting services are available.

435 rooms. High-speed Internet access. Two restaurants, two bars. Fitness room, fitness classes available, spa. Indoor pool, whirlpool. Airport transportation available. Business center. $$$$

W Chicago City Center ★★★☆☆

172 W. Adams St., Chicago, 312-332-1200, 888-625-5144;
www.whotels.com

Blending in perfectly in a decidedly urban setting in the city's financial district, this hotel provides a much-needed, hip hot-spot for locals and tourists alike. Old architecture of the former Midland Hotel mixes with modern accents in the W Living Room, where an after-work crowd mingles with drinks beneath the vaulted ceiling while listening to tunes spun by the DJ from a balcony above. Guest rooms are modern but comfortable, providing a respite from the commotion below. Dogs under 40 pounds are welcome here with a $100 fee and an extra $25 a night room charge. In exchange, you'll get attentive service, dog biscuits and more. Pets must be attended at all times. $$$

369 rooms. High-speed Internet access. Restaurant, two bars. Fitness room. Airport transportation available. Business center.

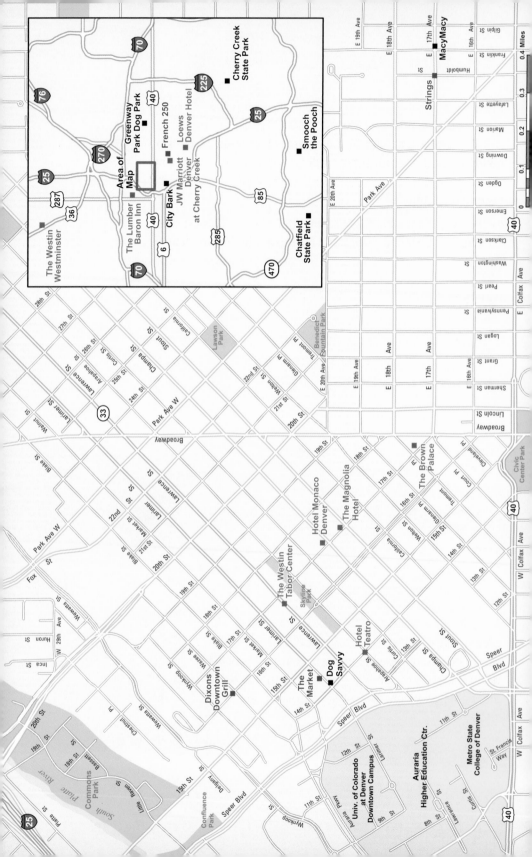

Denverites have never been shy when it comes to showering love on their four-legged friends. With the largest park system in the country, hundreds of miles of hiking trails, numerous pet-friendly events and pet-pampering emporiums, the Mile High City unabashedly demonstrates its devotion to animals.

In 2003, the Purina Pet Institute announced the healthiest cities for pets in the United States, and for those who live in Denver, it came as no surprise that their metropolis was ranked top dog, in large part because of the city's impressive veterinarian-to-pet ratio, easy access to emergency clinics and low flea population, which was the lowest of any city included in the survey.

Whether you want to take your pooch to a pool, shower your cat with house-made gourmet treats or unleash your hound at an off-leash dog park, Denver provides a perfect pet's life.

Chatfield State Park

Sit, Stay, See

11500 N. Roxborough Park Rd., Littleton;
303-470-1144, 800-678-226;
http://parks.state.co.us/Parks/Chatfield/

This beautiful state park, located south of Denver, has 75 acres of hiking trails, wide open spaces, and splashing areas for dogs and their energetic owners to run and roam free without the hindrance of leashes. The area sports a pond and two lakes conducive to swimming and stick-retrieving, along with picnicking areas for rest and relaxation. The park is not fenced, which means that you'll want to make sure your well-trained pooch knows to come bounding back when you call his name. Entry to the park is $6, or you can purchase an annual state parks pass if you plan to enjoy the grounds all summer long.

Cherry Creek State Park

4201 S. Parker Rd., Aurora,
http://parks.state.co.us/Parks/CherryCreek/

Dogs of all ages, breeds and attitudes frolic together at the southern end of this expansive park, which encompasses more than 60 fenced acres of off-leash running room. The area is open and grassy with natural prairie land and plenty of space to chase down a tennis ball, and there's also a small stream for water play. If your furry companion prefers a leisurely walk, the park trumpets 12 miles of trails coupled with gorgeous panoramic vistas of the Front Range. The park is also a haven for horseback riders, so make sure that your canine friend doesn't mistake a horse's hind legs for a tug-of-war toy. Daily admission is $7, May-September, $8 rest of the year, yearly pass is the same amount.

City Bark

370 Kalamath St., Denver, 303-573-9400; *www.citybark.com*

You spend countless hours scouring literature and Web sites to determine what day care is best for your toddler, so why shouldn't you invest the same amount of time investigating your doggie daycare options? City Bark makes the grade. It's the crème de le crème of overnight slumbering spots, complete with web-cams—which means that if you're traveling and have

access to the Internet, you can log on to see if your pooch is in the inner circle —or in time-out. Other amenities include grooming, dog walking, self-wash tubs, behavior training, a public dog park boasting a swimming pool, hills, tunnels and ample space to play fetch. All daycare dogs are required to pass an interview before joining their four-legged friends and proof of vaccinations is necessary.

Denver Dumb Friends League Furry Scurry

Washington Park, Denver,

303-751-5772; *www.ddfl.org*

A benefit for the Denver Dumb Friends League, the single largest canine event in Denver takes place every year, usually the first weekend in May, at Washington Park. The two-mile walk and fun-run attracts thousands of pet owners from all over the city who congregate early to secure their place in the romp. You can register on the day of the event, but preregistration is preferable. Snacks, drinks, breakfast bites and pet-friendly vendors are always on-site, and the pooch-pampering Hotel Teatro sponsors a Yappy Hour the night before the Scurry.

Dog Savvy

1402 Larimer St., Denver, 303-623-5200; *www.dogsavvy.com*

Situated in Larimer Square, one of Denver's hippest districts for humans, this posh pampering palace for canines fits perfectly into the fabric of the neighborhood. Showcasing a fantastic selection of up-to-the-minute sweaters, accessories, bejeweled collars, natural and organic treats and food, and cushy beds, your pooch will want for nothing. The swank boutique also features a luxurious doggie spa offering "pawdicures," self-serve baths using all-natural shampoos and conditioners, brushes and fluffs, aromatherapy, and "blueberry facials."

Greenway Park Dog Park

E. 24th Ave. and Syracuse St., Denver; *www.stapletondenver. com*

Far more gussied up than your average bark park, this fenced-in, well-manicured, tree-shaded park near the old Stapleton Airport is a bona fide social hound ground for well-behaved dogs and their devoted owners. Fire hydrants are scattered throughout the park (a nice touch); tennis balls are strewn here, there and everywhere for a pick-up game of catch; and dogs even have their very own water fountain (there's one for humans, too).

Smooch the Pooch

3624 E. Highlands Ranch Pkwy.,
Highlands Ranch,
303-346-8009;
www.smooch-thepooch.com

If Paris Hilton took up residence in Denver, this is where she would shop, thanks to the dashing designer duds, state-of-the-art doggie carriers and strollers, bold-hued jewelry, and snazzy collars and leads proffered at this trendy boutique. Shop 'til you drop and then leave your pooch to indulge in a luxe spa session—of which there are many. Popular with the posh crowds is the Pampered Pup Package, a hydro-massage bath customized to your pet's skin and coat, enhanced by a soothing balm paw treatment, nail trim, blow dry, brush out, bow or bandana, and a splash of perfume.

Strings ★★★☆☆

Chow time

1700 Humboldt St., Denver, 303-831-7310;
www.stringsrestaurant.com

Light and airy, mostly white with a red wall here and a brick one there, a kitchen open to view, and servers who seem unperturbed no matter what the request, Strings is like no other restaurant in Denver. The locals know it. So do scores of celebrities and politicians visiting the city, many of whom have left autographed pictures on the wall. The menu features hearty pastas, like bucatini with veal meatballs and plum tomato marinara. An outdoor patio is roomy enough for diners and pets.

American menu. Lunch, dinner. Bar. Business casual attire. Reservations recommended. Valet parking. Outdoor seating. $$$

Dixons Downtown Grill

1610 16th St., Denver, 303-573-6100; *www.dixonsrestaurant. com*

This casual American spot in Lower Downtown (LoDo) serves everything from Southwestern fish tacos to traditional fish and chips. Dogs are allowed on the patio, and friendly servers treat them to bowls of water and biscuits.

American menu. Breakfast, brunch, lunch, dinner.

French 250

250 Steele St., Denver, 303-331-0250; *www.french250.com*

Following in the paw steps of French tradition, this upscale French restaurant, in the heart of Cherry Creek, rolls out the red carpet for diners with dogs by offering a dog-walking service (for a fee) while you feast on foie gras and other Francophile favorites. A company called Poocharella oversees the service (303-564-1163 or *www.poocharella.com*).

French menu. Lunch, dinner, brunch.

The Market

1445 Larimer St., Denver, 303-534-5140; *www.themarketatlarimer.com*

Located in the heart of Larimer Square, this groovy European-styled coffee house allows pooches to perch with their humans on the outdoor patio. The truly vast menu includes sandwiches made to order and plenty of comfort food entrees, including roast turkey with stuffing or freshly made meatloaf.

Deli. Breakfast, lunch, dinner, late-night.

The Brown Palace Hotel ★★★★☆

321 17th St., Denver, 303-297-3511, 800-321-2599;
www.brownpalace.com

Denver's most celebrated and historic hotel, the Brown Palace has been hosting visitors since 1892, and many presidents, monarchs, and celebrities have graced its halls. The elegant lobby features a magnificent stained-glass ceiling, which tops off six levels of cast-iron balconies. The luxurious guest rooms have two styles, Victorian or Art Deco, both tastefully done. The award-winning Palace Arms restaurant features signature favorites like rack of lamb and pan-roasted veal. Cigar aficionados flock to the library ambience of the Churchill Bar, while the Ship Tavern appeals to lovers of the sea. Afternoon tea is accompanied by live harp music. Ellyngton's Sunday brunch is legendary and should not be missed. After a busy day of exploring nearby attractions like the 16th Street Mall and the Museum of Natural History, the full-service spa is the perfect place to

unwind with a deep massage, body treatment or facial. This hotel gives pets of all sizes a warm welcome with bowl and bed; dogs must be accompanied by a $75 fee and proof of registration and rabies vaccination.

241 rooms. High-speed, wireless Internet access. Three restaurants, bar. Spa. Business center. $$$

Hotel Monaco Denver ★★★☆☆

1717 Champa St., Denver, 303-296-1717, 800-990-1303; *www.monaco-denver.com*

Just how much fun can sophistication be? To find out, check in to this downtown hotel. Rooms with plush duvets, bathroom phones, 24-hour room service, terrycloth shower curtains, and turndown service remind you that the Monaco is as serious about service as it is about fun. Even your pet will think so when she is presented with her own food and water bowl, bag of gour-

met treats, and cushy bed—all at no extra cost for pets of any size. If you really want to go all out for your pet, the Monaco offers a "Reigning Cats and Dogs Pet Package," which includes organic treats, bottled water, your choice of a Pet Pamper Basket or four hours of dog sitting, a pooper scooper bag, and walking map. Don't forget to buy a yo-yo from your mini-bar before you check out.

189 rooms. High-speed, wireless Internet access. Restaurant. Fitness room, spa. Business center. $$$

Hotel Teatro ★★★☆☆

1100 14th St., Denver, 303-228-1100, 888-727-1200; *www.hotelteatro.com*

Tucked inside the historic Denver Tramway Building, this boutique hotel manages to respect its heritage while providing a thoroughly modern experience. Rooms include niceties like down comforters, Frette linens, Aveda bath products, and Starbucks coffee. The hotel even has Range Rovers to transport you around downtown. And don't think you're the only one who will be pampered here. The Teatro is extremely pet-friendly, providing quick walks at check-in, a dog menu, and a customized doggie dish with your pet's name on it and a bowl of Fiji water to lap. Best of all, there is no pet deposit fee.

111 rooms. High-speed, wireless Internet access. Two restaurants, bar. Fitness room. Business center. $$$

Loews Denver Hotel ★★★☆☆

4150 E. Mississippi Ave., Denver, 303-782-9300; 800-563-9712; *www.loewshotels.com*

Saying Loews is pet-friendly is like calling Denver a village. For a fee of $25, not only does Fido get his own bed, toy, and even a video, he gets a room service menu of veterinarian-approved items. Fortunately, the kids won't be jealous, since Loews offers Frisbees, backpacks and games for kids of all ages. And the hotel has a plethora of amenities for the littlest ones, from baby tubs and electric bottle warmers to tub faucet guards, rattles, and invisible outlet plugs. For mom and dad, there's a menu of "comfort items" like chenille throws, a selection of pillows, and CDs and a player. This isn't just a family hotel, though; business travelers will appreciate the on-site business center, fitness room, restaurant, and lounge.

183 rooms. High-speed, wireless Internet access. Restaurant, bar. Children's activity center. Fitness room. Business center. $$

The Lumber Baron Inn & Gardens

2555 W. 37th Ave., Denver, 303-477-8205, 888-214-2790; *www.lumberbaron.com*

This place is *big,* and there are only five guest rooms. The ground floor consists of a parlor, huge dining room, kitchen, and entertainment room with a 61-inch TV. The entire third floor is a big old ballroom. Doesn't every bed-and-breakfast have one? The Lumber Baron Inn was built in 1890 by an immigrant who made his considerable fortune in lumber (natch), and each

room of this mansion features a different wood—cherry, sycamore, oak, maple, poplar, and walnut. Rooms have separate showers and whirlpool tubs. And that third-floor ballroom, with its 20-foot vaulted ceiling, small kitchen, and bathroom? It's used for anything from a romantic dinner for two to the weekly murder mystery dinner hosted by the inn. Pets can stay with their owners in the renovated guest rooms, but they must be crated.

5 rooms. Complimentary full breakfast. $$

The Magnolia Hotel ★★★☆☆

818 17th St., Denver, 303-607-9000; 888-915-1110; *www.magnoliahoteldenver.com*

Many visitors to Denver make the Magnolia their home for extended stays, and it's easy to see why. Set back from busy 17th Street, the Magnolia says cozy from the wingback chairs and fireplace in its lobby to the full-size kitchens in its suites. Access to a snazzy health club is included with your stay. For a few dollars more, guests can use the Magnolia Club, which offers wireless Internet access, a nightly cocktail reception, continental breakfast, and late-night milk and cookies—just the thing after a day of high-powered business meetings. Guests don't have to leave their pets at home— pets are welcomed with a goodie bag at check-in.

246 rooms. Complimentary continental breakfast. High-speed, wireless Internet access. Restaurant, bar. Fitness room. Airport transportation available. Business center. $$$

The Westin Tabor Center ★★★☆☆

1672 Lawrence St., Denver, 303-572-9100, 800-937-8461; *www.westin.com*

Centrally located in downtown Denver and adjacent to the 16th Street Mall, this hotel boasts some of the largest guest rooms in the city, many with panoramic views of the Rocky Mountains. The Westin's signature Heavenly Beds (available for dogs, too) and Heavenly Baths, nightly wine service, appetizers, music, and optional massages ensure a relaxing stay. Canines weighing less than 30 pounds are welcome to stay with their owners if accompanied by a refundable deposit.

430 rooms. High-speed, wireless Internet access. Two restaurants, bar. Fitness room. Indoor pool, outdoor pool, whirlpool. Business center. $$$

The Westin Westminster ★★★☆☆

10600 Westminster Blvd., Westminster, 303-410-5000; 800-937-8461; *www.westin.com*

Located halfway between Boulder and Denver, just off Highway 36, the business-friendly Westin Westminster is an oasis on the high plains. Perched on Westminster's promenade, it's surrounded by shops, restaurants, a movie theater and the country's largest ice arena. Rustic but modern décor defines the public and private spaces. Pets are accepted with a deposit. The Westin's signature Heavenly Beds and Heavenly Dog Beds ensure that all guests get a good night's rest.

369 rooms. High-speed Internet access. Restaurant, bar. Children's activity center. Fitness room. Indoor pool, whirlpool. Business center. $

RODEO DR. ➡ BH 700

Angelenos love their pets, especially smaller pooches that double as fashion accessories—which means there are plenty of activities here for dog-owners and their furry friends. Start off with one of the many off-leash dog parks, like Silver Lake Dog Park. Take a break at nearby Back Door Bakery with croissants and doggy treats. Spend the afternoon shopping at the Grove, a large, glitzy outdoor shopping center in Beverly Hills, and pick up warm sweaters or statement T-shirts for the both of you. When it's time for some pampering, hop into a dog spa for fancy or holistic treatment.

Catts & Doggs Pet Boutique

Sit, Stay, See

2833 Hyperion Ave., Los Angeles, 323-953-8383

Catts and Doggs carries standard pet supplies like grooming goods, collars and books, as well as treats and food, many of which are all-natural and healthful for your pet. The 12-year-old boutique extends its holistic approach to its popular grooming treatments and packages.

Chateau Marmutt

8128 W. Third St., Los Angeles, 323-653-2062; *www.chateaumarmutt.com*

Even the most pet-friendly towns have some places that simply do not allow pets. So while you see the sights of tinseltown, park your pet at the best doggie day care in town. A playful pun on the famed Chateau Marmont hotel in West Hollywood, Chateau Marmutt is both a pet boutique and kennel, where the emphasis is on play and mingling with other mutts rather than staying put. Smaller dogs are separated from the larger ones, and all dogs must have proof of vaccinations. The

boutique has a vast selection of rhinestone collars, dog clothing, and even dog nail polish. Chateau Marmutt also provides aromatherapy dog grooming for $25 to $150 and "pawicures" for $10 to $20 dollars. Call in advance to make an appointment.

Le Pet Boutique

189 The Grove Dr., Los Angeles, 323-935-9195

Take your pet on a shopping spree at this boutique that sells a wide variety of clothing—its Halloween costumes are especially popular during the season. Their rhinestone collars are a hit among patrons, but you can also find more sedate and tasteful versions of collars and leashes.

Fifi & Romeo

7282 Beverly Blvd., Los Angeles, 323-857-7215; *http://fifiandromeo.com*

At this pet couture haven, you'll find Fifi & Romeo's signature cashmere sweaters, as well as its ultra-chic pet carriers—the best way to show off (or hide) your small pet. Fifi & Romeo's success has resulted in locations opening internationally, but the Los Angeles store is its headquarters. Other luxe items include bed throws and cashmere pillows.

My Pet Naturally

12001 W. Pico Blvd., Los Angeles, 310-477-3030, 877-469-7381; *Mypetnaturally.com*

This holistic store has a large apothecary with raw foods and other eco-friendly products like hemp beds, collars and leashes. There's even an on-site bakery that bakes many of the treats, like double-dipped bone cookies—and there's an espresso bar for pet owners. Sam's Yams—dehydrated, naturally sweet potato chews—are popular among patrons.

Runyon Canyon Park

2000 N. Fuller, off Mulholland Dr. near Rte. 101, Hollywood, *http://www.runyon-canyon.com*

Travelers with a yen for a workout during their stay in Los Angeles will love Runyon Canyon's dog park and hiking trails. Nestled in the hills of Hollywood, dogs and their walkers are bound to meet similar company at this popular park famous for its scenic hikes. Visitors can enter the park through several entrances at Mulholland Drive and Vista Street, but the easiest route is by starting at the bottom of the canyon at Fuller Avenue. From there, trek up the gravelly road to reach Clouds Rest and Inspiration Point—areas where the trail plateaus and many hikers savor a sunrise or sunset and a view of Hollywood

below. On a clear day, the Pacific Ocean, Catalina Island and the Hollywood sign are visible. Runyon Canyon also has an off-leash section for dogs that love to run free. Don't be surprised if you spot celebrities on the trails—Runyon Canyon Park is a favorite haunt of stars and their pets. The park also boasts what remains of a Frank Lloyd Wright-designed pool pavilion.

Venice Beach Boardwalk

1800 Ocean Front Walk, Venice, 310-822-5425 (Venice Beach Chamber of Commerce), 888-527-2757 (L.A. Parks)

Los Angeles' west side is fringed with a stretch of sandy beaches, but it's Venice that continues to attract locals, their dogs, and a steady flow of bikers, rollerbladers and joggers. Dogs aren't allowed to frolic on the beach, but they are more than welcome to stroll along Venice's famous boardwalk, where visitors can browse the stalls of the colorful vendors who sell everything from piles of sage to handcrafted jewelry. Bright murals, carica-ture artists, roasted corn hot off the grill and henna tattoo stands give Venice Beach its unique character. Dogs are restricted from the boardwalk on Fridays, Saturdays and Sundays after 11 a.m. because of the increased flow of bikers and joggers, but your pup is welcome all day during the week.

Toast Bakery Cafe ★☆☆☆☆

8221 W. Third St., Los Angeles, 323-655-5018;
www.toastbakerycafe.net

Indulge your craving for cool at this Beverly Hills café, which serves American fare with some flare, like fancy grilled cheese sandwiches with mozzarella, feta cheese and sun-dried tomatoes. Items from the bakery are sure to satisfy a sweet tooth, including the popular red velvet cake. There's also a full breakfast menu and plentiful outdoor seating for you and your pet, who can sip from a bowl of water.

Abbot's Habit

1401 Abbot Kinney Blvd., Venice, 310-399-1171

Located on the main artery of Venice, this café serves coffee, made-to-order sandwiches and Italian subs, as well as pastries from local bakeries. Outdoor seating accommodates not only your dog but also any people-watching urges. If you drop by on a Friday, you might even catch an open mic night.

Back Door Bakery

1710 Silver Lake Blvd., Los Angeles, 323-662-7927

Everything is made from scratch at this popular bakery and breakfast spot, including the ketchup, mayonnaise and jams. It's conveniently located next to off-leash Silver Lake Dog Park, making it easy to grab a croissant or omelet after a morning walk.

Cat & Fiddle

6530 W. Sunset Blvd., Los Angeles, 323-468-3800; *http://thecatandfiddle.com*

This 22-year-old British pub has people coming back for its beautiful outdoor patio, where customers often bring their pooches. Dogs can sip on water while you get a drink or enjoy your meal—the shepherd's pie and bangers and mash are popular dishes.

British menu. Lunch, dinner, late-night. Bar.

Lazy Daisy Cafe

2300 Pico Blvd., Santa Monica, 310-450-9011

This Santa Monica location of this laidback café serves organic coffee with its breakfast and café lunch staples (think eggs benedict and hearty sandwiches). Dogs are allowed on the outside patio, and bowls of water are available upon request.

Mäni's on Fairfax

519 S. Fairfax Ave., Los Angeles, 323-938-8800;
www.manisbakery.com

This bakery and café may serve a caramelized apple dish made from alternative sweeteners and vegan carrot cake, but it's not just for those with dietary restrictions. Nosh on a health-conscious sandwich or salad, try a fresh-baked pie, or grab breakfast, which is served all day. Enjoy the popular turkey chili with your pet on the outdoor patio. A water bowl can be provided.

American menu. Breakfast, lunch, dinner, late-night. Outdoor seating.

Prana Cafe

650 N. La Cienega Blvd., Los Angeles, 310-360-0551;
www.pranacafela.com

Enjoy Prana Cafe's Asian-influenced American dishes on the large outdoor seating area as your dog munches on doggie biscuits and sips water. It's located around the corner from Melrose Place, which means there's minimal smog to inhale as you dine on your Korean- or Thai-scrambled eggs. Or choose a soup, salad or sandwich from the complete lunch menu.

American, pan-Asian menu. Breakfast, lunch.

Lie Down

The Beverly Hills Hotel ★★★★★

9641 Sunset Blvd., Beverly Hills, 310-276-2251, 800-650-1842;
www.beverlyhillshotel.com

This deliciously pink iconic hotel oozes Hollywood glamour. Deals have been made here for decades and it has long been a hideaway for stars, who like to stay in the bungalows privately tucked away along the paths of lush gardens. The hotel maintains the allure of 1940s Hollywood in both its public and private rooms. The guest rooms and suites are decorated in soothing sage, yellow and beige and are furnished with canopied beds with matelasse comforters and velvet throw pillows. Fireplaces add a romantic touch, and terraces and balconies focus attention on the gardens. The restaurants, including the classic Polo Lounge and the recently opened Sunset Bar, still attract producers and stars, but visitors in the know head for the pool, where the scene is best viewed from a fantastic private cabana. Guests with pets of up to 35 pounds are welcome in this legendary hotel but are limited to the bungalow rooms and suites, located near the hotel's garden. There, your dog will receive star treatment with a dog bed, customized dog biscuits and pink tennis balls for a nonrefundable fee of $200.

204 rooms. High-speed, wireless Internet access. Restaurant, bar. Business center. $$$$

Chateau Marmont ★★★☆☆

8221 Sunset Blvd., Hollywood, 323-656-1010;
www.chateaumarmont.com

If walls could talk, there's no telling what you'd hear at this leg-

endary hotel. Known as the place where celebrities misbehave, it's as close to the action as you can probably get. The poolside people-watching may be worth the room price alone. Upon check-in, guests with dogs receive a kit that includes a doggie treat, water bowl and a dog bed. Dogs are also welcome in the hotel's restaurant. Guests with dogs must pay a $100 flat fee during their stay, but there is no limit on the size, weight or number of pets.

63 rooms. High-speed, wireless Internet access.Restaurant. $$$

Four Seasons Hotel Los Angeles at Beverly Hills ★★★★☆

300 S. Doheny Dr., Beverly Hills, 310-273-2222,800-819-5053; *www.fourseasons.com*

Located on a quiet palm-lined street only one mile from the exclusive boutiques of Rodeo Drive and Robertson Boulevard, this hotel is a wonderful retreat. Guest rooms include Frette linens and oversize marble bathrooms with Bulgari toiletries. The rooftop pool is surrounded by lush gardens and dotted with private cabanas. Don't miss the marvelous sunset massage from a candlelit cabana. Gardens restaurant features California-style cuisine with Latin American and Asian influences. Complimentary limo rides to shopping and restaurants are available. Travelers with dogs can stay at the hotel for no extra charge under the condition that the pet weigh less than 15 pounds and be supervised when in the guest room. Dog bowls and treats are provided.

285 rooms. High-speed, wireless Internet access. Three restaurants, bar. Spa. $$$$

Hyatt Regency Century Plaza
★★★☆☆

2025 Avenue of the Stars, Los Angeles, 310-228-1234; 800-554-9288; *www.hyatt.com*

Enveloped by lush tropical gardens, this contemporary hotel has guest rooms with balconies offering views of the Los Angeles cityscape and the tree-lined boulevards of Beverly Hills. Be sure to fit in a treatment at the Spa Mystique, which uses feng shui design principles in its 27 treatment rooms and four outdoor cabanas. Expect to pay $30 a night if you have a pet as a travel companion. The Hyatt also offers room service for dogs, with all-natural dishes such as the Buddy Burger, Bacon Pancake, and for dessert, the Barkin' Biscotti. The Gold Pawsport Frequent Pet Stay Program entitles your travel companion to many extras.

726 rooms. Restaurant, two bars. $$$

Hotel Bel-Air ★★★★★

701 Stone Canyon Rd., Los Angeles,
310-472-1211, 800-648-4097;
www.hotelbelair.com

This timeless hotel, close to the action of Los Angeles, has 12 acres of gardens. The luxurious guest rooms are spread throughout the grounds, giving guests privacy. Amenities include Kiehl's bath products in the tasteful guest rooms and a well-equipped fitness center. Travelers with pets do have to pay a hefty fee—pets weighing less than 25 pounds can stay with a $500 non-refundable clean-up tariff. They receive bowls, organic food, bottled water, and (for cats) a litter box.

91 rooms. High-speed, wireless Internet access. Restaurant, bar. $$$$

Le Montrose Suite Hotel ★★★☆☆

900 Hammond St., West Hollywood, 310-855-1115;
800-776-0666; *www.lemontrose.com*

The Art Nouveau-styled Le Montrose includes spacious suites with sunken living rooms, fireplaces and refrigerators, and many have kitchenettes and private balconies. Venture up to the roof for a dip in the pool and Jacuzzi or play a set on the tennis court. The noteworthy restaurant, the Library, is reserved exclusively for guests and their friends. For a $100 fee, dogs under 50 pounds are welcome at the hotel. Doggie bowls and a list of pet-friendly restaurants are available upon request.

133 rooms, all suites. High-speed Internet access. Restaurant. $$

Loews Santa Monica Beach Hotel ★★★☆☆

1700 Ocean Ave., Santa Monica,
310-458-6700, 866-563-9792;
www.loewshotels.com

Enjoy magnificent sunset views from this very SoCal beachfront haven. You'll feel very chic as you don the doeskin robe in the guest rooms, lounge at the striking ocean-front pool and bliss-out in the luxurious spa—a favorite of West Side-dwelling celebrities. The pet-friendly hotel charges $25 per pet with no restrictions. Pet amenities such as a food dish, treats and water bowls are included, and dog beds are available upon request.

342 rooms. Restaurant, two bars. Spa. Beach. $$$$

Sofitel Los Angeles ★★★☆☆

8555 Beverly Blvd., Los Angeles, 310-278-5444,
800-763-4835; *www.sofitel.com*

Fresh from a multi-million dollar renovation in 2006, this European-style hotel located across

from the Beverly Center includes comfy rooms with rain showers and fresh flowers. Two trendy restaurants top off the experience. Free shuttle service to the airport and Union Station is available. Guests with dogs of all weights and sizes pay no extra fees and are offered a dog bowl and dog treats. Depending on availability and the dog's size, a dog bed is available.

297 rooms, all suites. High-speed Internet access. Restaurants, bar. $$$

Viceroy ★★★☆☆

1819 Ocean Ave., Santa Monica, 310-260-7500, 800-670-6185; *www.viceroysantamonica.com*

You'll feel like part of the cool crowd at this beach hotel. The hotel's fashionably retro Cameo Bar is where the city's beautiful people mingle and the award-winning restaurant, Whist, serves a killer Sunday Champagne brunch. Best of all is the famed cabana-ringed pool. Afterward, you can retreat to your stunning guest room (decorated by celeb designer Kelly Wearstler) for spa treatments by Fred Segal Beauty. You get the picture. Dogs 40 pounds and under are allowed for a one-time $50 fee, with dog bowls, treats and bed provided. The hotel also offers a convenient list of dog-friendly things to do in Los Angeles.

162 rooms. High-speed, wireless Internet access. Restaurant, bar. $$$$

The Westin Bonaventure Hotel and Suites
★★★☆☆

404 S. Figueroa St., Los Angeles,
213-624-1000; 800-937-8461;
www.westin.com

This mega-hotel, divided into five gleaming metal towers, is like a city unto itself. Enter the six-story lobby and wind through the indoor gardens and waterfalls to one of 12 elevators that whisk you to your pie-shaped room; all rooms feature an entire wall of windows overlooking the city. To cap it off, there's a rooftop steakhouse and revolving lounge. Guests with pets do not have to pay a fee but dogs must weigh less than 40 pounds. The Bonaventure also provides the signature, extra cushiony "Heavenly" dog beds.

1,354 rooms. High-speed Internet access. Three restaurants, two bars. $$$

News Café ★★☆☆☆

800 Ocean Dr., Miami Beach, 305-538-6397; *www.newscafe.com*

This spot on Ocean Drive in South Beach regularly makes the news with A-list celebrity sightings, although the news in the name officially refers to an in-house bookstore and newsstand. In addition to salads, soups, sandwiches, pizzas and a smattering of Middle Eastern dishes, such as falafel and tabbouleh salad, the café serves breakfast round-the-clock. Most (and the best) seating is outside with plenty of Ocean Drive people-watching, and room for pets.

International menu. Breakfast, lunch, dinner, late-night. Bar. Casual attire. Valet parking. Outdoor seating. $$

Fairmont Turnberry Isle Resort & Club ★★★★☆

Lie Down

19999 W. Country Club Dr., Aventura, 305-933-6937, 800-257-7544; *www.fairmont.com*

Located near Fort Lauderdale in Aventura, Turnberry Isle completed a $100 million dollar renovation in 2006, transforming its 300 perfectly manicured acres along the Atlantic Ocean into the likes of a palatial private estate. Four restaurants and five lounges take their cue from the ocean-front location with superb seafood and continental dishes. Two Robert Trent Jones, Sr. golf courses prove challenging and inspiring, while the famous Island Green 18th hole continues to bewitch golfers. Turnberry's two tennis centers are often counted among the country's best. Pets up to 20 pounds are accepted here with a $25 per day fee. The hotel offers a pet menu with freshly made and commercial food and bowls and leashes for sale and loan. Dogs receive a free Fairmont-engraved dog tag, chew toy, treats and toothbrush.

392 rooms. Four restaurants, five bars. Fitness room, spa. Indoor pool. Golf. Tennis. Business center. $$$$

Fontainebleau Miami Beach ★★★☆☆

4441 Collins Ave., Miami Beach, 305-538-2000, 800-548-8886; *www.fontainebleau.com*

This Miami Beach landmark is a three-building resort sitting on 20 tropical acres. With 190,000 square feet of meeting space, it is a major business destination, but not without significant draws for leisure travelers, like the half-acre multi-pool with waterfalls. Pets of any size are accepted with a $75 fee.

1,328 rooms. High-speed Internet access. Two restaurants, two bars. Children's activity center. Fitness room. Beach. Outdoor pool, children's pool, whirlpool. Business center. $$

Four Seasons Hotel Miami ★★★★☆

1435 Brickell Ave., Miami, 305-358-3535, 800-819-5053; *www.fourseasons.com*

This contemporary, sleek hotel is conveniently located in downtown Miami's newly buzzing Brickell neighborhood. Guest rooms and suites are serene spaces decorated with cool earth tones and distinctive artwork. Service at the Four Seasons is polished and professional, especially at the skyline-level pool,

where attendants tend to guests with water spritzes and cool towels. The 50,000-square-foot Splash Spa at the onsite Sports Club/LA has 10 treatment rooms and a unique menu of offerings. The hotel features a fine-dining restaurant, Acqua, which serves up Latin-inspired fare, and two lounges, including the poolside Bahia where locals and travelers alike gather for cocktails. Dogs and cats up to 15 pounds are accepted without a fee. Bowls and pet food are available.

305 rooms. High-speed Internet access. Restaurant, two bars. Children's activity center. Fitness room, fitness classes available, spa. Outdoor pool, children's pool, whirlpool. Airport transportation available. Business center. $$$

Grand Bay Miami
★★★☆☆

2669 S. Bayshore Dr., Miami,
www.grandbaymiami.com

This tropical getaway provides a great location in stylish Coconut Grove near downtown Miami. Pastel colors and a breezy elegance define the interior of this resort. Java addicts line up at the resort's on-site Starbucks, while jet-setters head to Bice, one of the top restaurants in town. Whether you're seeking a reservation at a nearby restaurant or booking an off-site adventure, the concierge service is highly regarded. Pets of any size are accepted with a $20 per day fee.

177 rooms. High-speed Internet access. Restaurant, bar. Fitness room. Outdoor pool, whirlpool. Business center. $$$

Loews Miami Beach Hotel ★★★★☆

1601 Collins Ave., Miami Beach, 305-604-1601, 866-563-9792; *www.loewshotels.com*

With its beachfront location in the historic Art Deco district, the Loews Miami Beach Hotel is the perfect home base for sampling the dynamic restaurants, clubs and shops of Miami's South Beach. Its architecture blends an Art Deco landmark, the St. Moritz hotel, with new construction to form a thoroughly modern hotel. The hotel's pool is famous for its see-and-be-seen reputation, while the guest rooms are decorated

in the soothing hues of sun, sand and sea. Celeb chef Emeril Lagasse gives the seafood-heavy menu at his on-site restaurant, Emeril's South Beach, a Creole accent. Pets of any size are accepted without a fee. All furry guests receive a welcome bag with treats, food and water bowls; dog and cat in-room menus; use of the on-site dog-walking area with its own "dog food bar" and loaner collars, leashes, brushes, blankets, and toys.

790 rooms. High-speed Internet access. Three restaurants, three bars. Children's activity center. Fitness room, fitness classes available, spa. Beach. Outdoor pool, whirlpool. Airport transportation available. Business center.

Mandarin Oriental, Miami ★★★★☆

500 Brickell Key Dr., Miami, 305-913-8288, 866-526-6567; *www.mandarinoriental.com*

With its waterfront location, award-winning spa, and contemporary interior design, this hotel is an island of calm in the middle of downtown Miami. And we mean that literally. Located on tiny Brickell Key opposite the city center, this outpost of the famed Asian hotel group is a favorite among Miamians for its skyline views, Azul restaurant and its man-made white-sand beach. Those who prefer the real thing can sign up for the hotel's South Beach Experience, which includes transportation to South Beach, a private beach cabana, and access to the pool and restaurant at the famed Casa Casuarina. After the beach, retreat to one of the luxuriously appointed guest rooms decorated in a contemporary Asian-influenced style with bamboo hardwood floors, simple furnishings, and white fabrics. Pets up to 30 pounds are accepted with a $200 deposit ($100 of which is refundable). Bowls, pet beds, complimentary pet food and logo pet tags are provided. The hotel even offers "pet turndown" service with pet soap and candies.

327 rooms. High-speed Internet access. Two restaurants, two bars. Fitness room, fitness classes available, spa. Beach. Outdoor pool, whirlpool. Airport transportation available. Business center.

Raleigh Miami Beach ★★☆☆☆

1775 Collins Ave., Miami Beach, 305-534-6300, 800-848-1775, *www.raleighhotel.com*

Trendsetting hotelier Andre Balasz of the Standard Hotel in Los Angeles acquired the Art Deco Raleigh Hotel, which he

refurbished and reopened in 2004 to acclaim. Although it's located firmly in the midst of the South Beach nightlife circuit, only guests can take full advantage of the hotel's charms, including tropical-modern guest rooms, terrace suites and a keyhole-shaped pool where Esther Williams once performed water ballets. The see-and-be-seen set pose photo shoot-ready on the outdoor dining deck lit by globe lanterns. Pets of any size are accepted with a $100 fee.

104 rooms. High-speed, wireless Internet access. Three restaurants, three bars. Beach. Outdoor pool. Airport transportation available. $$$

The Ritz-Carlton, South Beach ★★★★☆

1 Lincoln Rd., Miami Beach, 786-276-4000, 800-542-8680; *www.ritzcarlton.com*

Mid-century modern meets 21st-century luxury at the Ritz-Carlton, South Beach. This landmark property, originally designed by legendary Miami architect Morris Lapidus, boasts an ideal location at the foot of South Beach's Lincoln Road Mall on the Atlantic Ocean. Rooms feature nautical hues, views of the ocean, and luxury touches like marble baths and feather-topped beds. The 16,000-square-foot La Maison de Beaute Carita spa is the centerpiece of the resort. Dining choices abound here, including restaurants that feature Caribbean, New American, and Floridian cuisine served in a variety of elegant and informal settings. Pets under 35 pounds are accepted with a $250 fee. The hotel provides four-poster dog beds with Italian sheets, designer collars, Evian or Fiji water, an in-room dog treat menu, and dog spa treatments (including grooming, massage and color).

376 rooms. High-speed Internet access. Four restaurants, four bars. Children's activity center. Fitness room, spa. Beach.

Outdoor pool, whirlpool. Airport transportation available. Business center.

The Tides Hotel ★★★☆☆

1220 Ocean Dr., Miami Beach, 305-604-5070, 800-439-4095; *www.thetideshotel.com*

Modern elegance abounds in this cream-and-white-themed contemporary hotel where the best suite will cost you $3,000 per night and bring all the luxury and pampering you'd expect at a high-class hotel. Renovated by John Pringle, every one of the elegant rooms overlooks the beach. Step out the front door, and you're just minutes away from the fine dining, shopping, art galleries, theaters and nightclubs that make South Beach famous. Pets up to 35 pounds are accepted with a $150 fee, which will get you the use of down pet beds; Burberry bowls, leashes and collars; litter box (for cats); treats; 24-hour pet-walking service; grooming; and in-room pet menu.

45 rooms, all suites. High-speed, wireless Internet access. Restaurant, two bars. Fitness room. Outdoor pool. Business center. $$$$

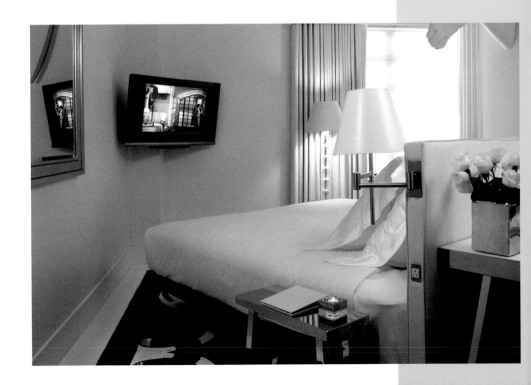

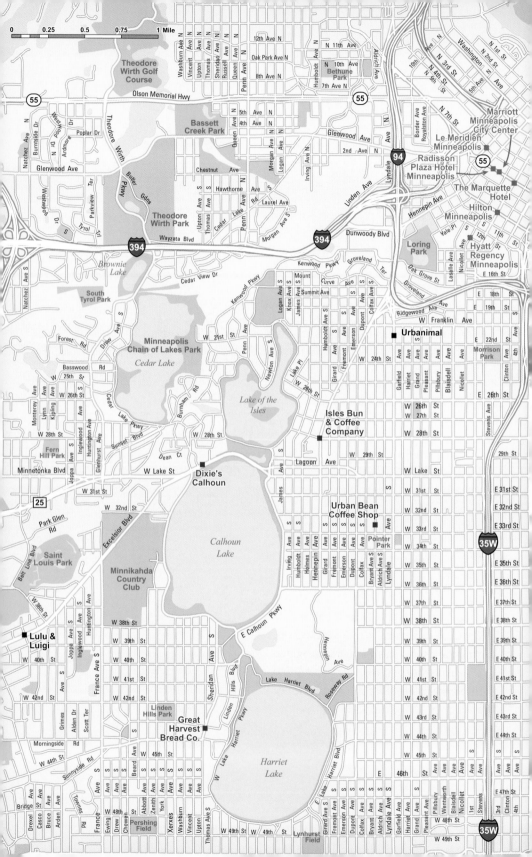

Minneapolis

Though much of the year is downright chilly in the Twin Cities, there's plenty to do indoors and out in this pet-friendly town. Warm weather brings miles of paths around the city's scores of lakes and plenty of outdoor dining on pet-friendly patios. During colder months, the city's famed covered skybridge system means you can walk for miles without ever having to go outside.

Chain of Lakes

Sit, Stay, See

Minneapolis Park and Recreation Board, Minneapolis, 612-230-6400; *www.minneapolisparks.org.*

When not walking the dog is simply not an option, the Minneapolis Chain of Lakes is where it's at. Clear, well-traveled, well-populated paths (over 13 miles) around the chain's lakes—Calhoun, Isles, Harriet, and Cedar and Brownie—are perfect for pet walking, not to mention running, in-line skating and other outdoor activities. The lakes, popular attractions year-round, are readily accessible from downtown Minneapolis.

Loring Park

Maple St. and Harmon Place, Minneapolis

For a quick romp with your pet in the city, visit any of five off-leash parks. The newest, and closest to downtown, is Loring Park Off-Leash Play Area, which was recently expanded and beautified with plenty of landscaping, boulders for climbing, trash receptacles and free pick-up bags. Dogs must have a license and a park permit to use off-leash areas, available from Animal Control, 212 17th Ave. N., Minneapolis, 612-348-4250.

LuLu & Luigi

3844 Grand Way, St. Louis Park, 952-929-1200;
www.luluandluigi.com

This boutique, run by a mother-and-daughter team, offers a vast selection of pet coats, boots, collars, leashes and more. Been searching for a vintage-look iron day bed for your pooch? This shop stocks them, plus stylish carriers, all-natural treats and catnip-filled cat toys. The suburban Wayzata location has a grooming "pawlour" that offers services from shampoos to pet-a-cures.

Urbanimal

2106 Lyndale Ave. S., Minneapolis, 612-879-0709;
www.urbanimal.com

This funky pet boutique stocks a full range of natural foods and supplements for dogs and cats, plus litter, bedding, accessories and more. Locals rave about the food delivery and pet care services and drop by often to nuzzle the shop's resident dogs and cats.

Great Harvest Bread Co.

4314 Upton Ave. S., Minneapolis, 612-929-2899;

www.greatharvestmn.com

This bakery and deli in Linden Hills is known for its delicious breads, cookies and soups. The friendly staff will dole out home-made dog bones to eager pups who come with their owners.

Chow Time

Isles Bun & Coffee Company

1424 W. 28th St., Minneapolis, 612-870-4466

Located in the Uptown section of Minneapolis, this coffee shop offers complimentary doggie treats to pets who join their owners for a morning cup of joe and pastry. The warm cinnamon rolls here are superb (regulars know to ask for extra frosting), and the location is within walking distance of lovely Lake of the Isles.

Urban Bean Coffee Shop

3255 Bryant Ave. S., Minneapolis, 612-824-6611

This funky coffee shop has plenty of outdoor tables where you can have a strong cup of coffee and a brownie while your pet is tempted with water and treats.

Graves 601 Hotel ★★★☆☆

Lie Down

601 First Ave. N., Minneapolis, 612-677-1100, 866-523-1100;

http://graves601hotel.com

Housed in a 22-story theater district building, this contemporary hotel has a sleek, minimalist lobby, stylish restaurant and rooms filled with luxury amenities. Bathrooms feature rain showers, limestone and Hermes bath products, while bedrooms have plush beds, plasma TVs and high speed internet access. The onsite restaurant, Cosmos, serves sophisticated food like vanilla butter lobster with sweet onion risotto. The hotel accepts small pets for a $150 fee.

255 rooms. High-speed Internet access. Restaurant, bar. Fitness room. Airport transportation available. Business center.

Hilton Minneapolis ★★★☆☆

1001 Marquette Ave. S., Minneapolis, 612-376-1000, 800-445-8667; *www.hiltonminneapolis.com*

This hotel is connected by skyway to the Minneapolis Convention Center and is near Orchestra Hall, the Guthrie Theater, great shopping and dining options, and more. The attractive guest rooms are nicely furnished and feature wireless Internet access,

plasma televisions, and upscale granite bathrooms. After a busy day at the office or enjoying the sites, take advantage of the indoor pool and whirlpool or the well-appointed fitness center. Pets up to 35 pounds are welcome without a fee.

821 rooms. High-speed, wireless Internet access. Restaurant, bar. Fitness room. Indoor pool, whirlpool. Business center.

Hyatt Regency Minneapolis ★★★☆☆

1300 Nicollet Mall, Minneapolis, 612-370-1234, 800-633-7313; *www.minneapolis.hyatt.com*

Located in the business and financial districts, this hotel offers access to the Minneapolis Convention Center via the city's skywalk system. The attractive guest rooms include the "Grand Bed"—a plush bed piled high with pillows and crisp linens—and contemporary bathrooms that feature granite floors and countertops. The hotel has an indoor pool and fitness center with a full-size basketball court, group classes and state-of-the-art machines. Small pets are accepted but there are some restrictions.

533 rooms. High-speed, wireless Internet access. Two restaurants, bar. Fitness room, fitness classes available. Indoor pool. Airport transportation available. Business center.

Rebecca Taylor and Nanette Lepore. Feel free to bring your dog with you to get his opinion on what you should wear.

Bongo Java

2007 Belmont Blvd., Nashville, 615-385-5282

This laidback Nashville coffee house located near Belmont University is a favorite of the many regulars who come to linger over their brews with their pets at their feet on the huge outdoor deck. Locals rave about the variety of bagel sandwiches, wraps and other snacks. Live music is often performed in the upstairs space.

Coffee house. Breakfast, lunch, dinner.

Eastland Café

97 Chapel Ave., Nashville, 615-627-1088;
www.eastlandcafe.com

Locals love this casual, but creative eatery, which takes Southern food to a new level. But the attraction for dog owners is Lappy Hour (*www.nashville-lappyhour.com*), a regular gathering on the patio outdoors during the summer. The restaurant also hosts Oktoberfest and other annual events.

American, Southern menu. Casual attire. Dinner. Bar. Closed Sunday. Outdoor seating.

Jack's Bar-B-Que

416 Broadway, Nashville,
615-254-5715;
www.jacksbarbque.com

Head to the back of the building for the outdoor seating area, where dogs are welcome to join their owners for a tasty slab of meat. The downtown

location is close to LP Field, where the Titans play, and overlooks the legendary Ryman Auditorium.

American menu. Casual attire. Lunch, dinner. Outdoor seating.

Jackson's Bar and Bistro

1800 21st Ave. S., Nashville, 615-385-9968

This might look like just the usual college-area ultra-hip coffee shop, bar and bistro. But a larger-than-average patio accommodates plenty of pups. The staff (many Vanderbilt students) loves dogs and will be sure to fill—and refill—your dog's water bowl quickly.

American menu. Casual attire. Breakfast, lunch, dinner, late-night. Bar. Outdoor seating.

I Dream of Weenie

1108 Woodland St., Nashville

You'll pass it the first time you drive by, because this hot dog vendor serves from a glorified food cart. But the cart serves up tasty speciality hot dogs, and there is plenty of curb space and grassy spots on which to sit. Open for lunch.

Sip Café

1402 McGavock Pike, Nashville, 615-227-1035

This neighborhood coffee shop couldn't be friendlier, to dogs as well as to people. The ample patio in back is shared by the neighboring Castrillo's Pizza, a used bookstore and a dog-watering fountain. No reason not to sit and sip for a while.

Lie Down

The Hermitage Hotel ★★★★★

231 Sixth Ave. N., Nashville, 615-244-3121; 888-888-9414 ; *www.thehermitagehotel.com*

The Hermitage Hotel is the pride of Nashville. Opened in 1910, this downtown hotel recalls the grace and charm of a former time. The spacious guest rooms feature down duvet-topped

beds, marble bathrooms, and DVD and CD players. With 24-hour room service, there's no need to leave. Those who do stop in at the onsite Capitol Grille are treated to perfectly prepared dishes such as beef tenderloin with pears, argula, and parsnips. The adjacent Oak Bar, with its emerald green club chairs and dark wood paneling, is a top spot for drinks before or after dinner. Dogs of any size are welcome. There is a $25 per night fee for bringing a dog with you, but she will be treated with style, including custom pet beds and a special room service menu.

122 rooms. High-speed, wireless Internet access. Restaurant, bar. Fitness room, fitness classes available, spa. Business center. $$$

Hotel Indigo Nashville West End

1719 West End Ave., Nashville, 615-329-4200, 877 846 3446; *www.ichotelsgroup.com*

Crisp and contemporary, this West End boutique hotel has

rooms with duvet-topped beds, flat-screen TVs and CD players. Spacious suites provide even more room to spread out, while kitchens equipped with full-size fridges and coffee makers make lingering awhile a possibility. Pets are welcome with the payment of a $150 one-time, nonrefundable fee.

139 rooms. High-speed, wireless Internet. Fitness center. Restaurant. $$

Hotel Preston ★★★☆☆

733 Briley Parkway, Nashville, 615-361-5900;
www.hotelpreston.com

This stylish spot is more city chic than cowboy country, though Opryland and all of the city's famous places are within easy reach. The guestrooms and suites blend sophistication with a bit of whimsy—you can get everything from a lava lamp to a pet fish, art kit and even a rubber ducky upon check-in. Café Isabella whips up Italian favorites with a dash of Southern spirit (think baked ziti and chicken pot pie), while the trendy Pink

Slip bar provides libations and live, local music. The hotel is pet friendly, and welcomes animals for a $49 non-refundable fee, which includes water and food dishes, toys and snacks.

190 rooms. High-speed, wireless Internet access. Restaurant, bar. Fitness room, spa. Outdoor pool. Airport transportation available. Business center. $$$

Loews Vanderbilt Hotel Nashville ★★★☆☆

2100 West End Ave., Nashville,
615-320-1700, 866-563-9792; *www.loewshotels.com*

This upscale property is conveniently located in the heart of the Vanderbilt district between the university and downtown. Comfortable guest rooms, which offer views of either the campus or city, feature quality bedding, minibars, plush robes and Bloom toiletries. The works of Harold Kraus, a renowned Nashville artist, are featured on-site at the Kraus Gallery. Loews hotels are known for being among the most pet-friendly, and the Vanderbilt is no exception. If you forget a collar, leash, dog bed

or any other essential, they'll have one on hand you can borrow. The room service menu offers dishes such as "bow wow tenderloin of beef" and "chowhound chicken." You can also grab a list of good dog-walking routes from the front desk.

340 rooms. High-speed Internet access. Two restaurants, two bars. Children's activity center. Fitness room, spa. Airport transportation available. Business center. $$

Sheraton Music City ★★★☆☆

777 McGavock Pike, Nashville, 615-885-2200; 800-325-3535; *www.sheratonmusiccity.com*

This property is designed to look like a Deep South mansion. It's convenient to Nashville proper—located three miles from the airport, five miles from Opry Mills, and seven miles from downtown. Dogs up to 80 pounds are welcome guests in the first-floor rooms, and no extra deposit is required.

410 rooms. Restaurant, bar. Fitness room. Indoor pool, outdoor pool, children's pool, whirlpool. Tennis. Airport transportation available. Business center. $$

Sheraton Nashville Downtown Hotel ★★★☆☆

623 Union St., Nashville, 615-259-2000, 800-325-3535;
www.sheraton-nashville.com

This contemporary hotel is situated in the heart of downtown Nashville near the capitol building. Guests are offered a host of amenities and services that make a stay here not only pleasant but pampering. Room service, turndown service, television with cable, coffee makers, plush bathrobes, and Sheraton's signature plush beds offer true relaxation in the guest rooms, while the concierge offers carefree planning for both business and leisure needs. Pets are welcome guests here with no extra deposit required, but you must sign a waiver at check-in.

476 rooms. High-speed, wireless Internet access. Restaurant, bar. Fitness room, spa. Indoor pool. Business center. $$

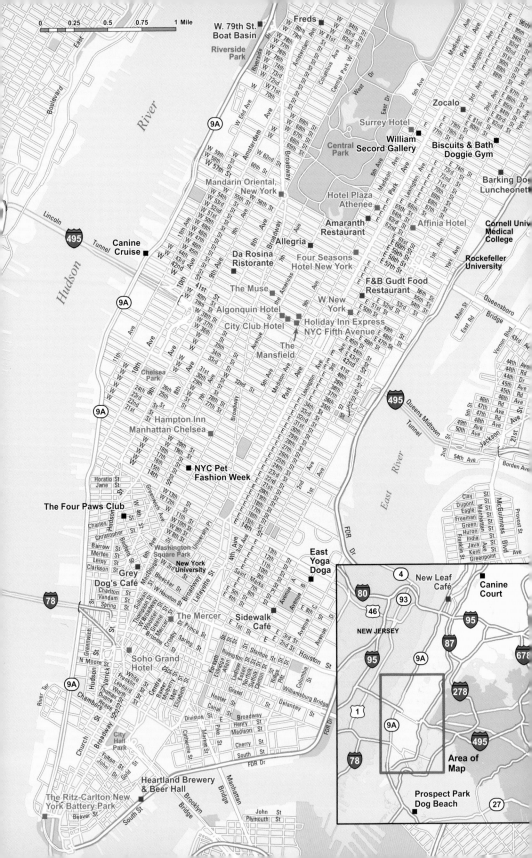

New York

The Big Apple is a pooch's paradise with plenty of pet-friendly hotels, restaurants and activities to enjoy. From canine cruises up the Hudson River to well-deserved pampering at some of the city's finest boutique hotels, no destination could be finer for pets (and their owners) than New York City. The warmer months allow for great al fresco noshing and walks along New York's numerous boardwalks (just be sensitive to the hot dogs at Coney Island). As the weather cools, get a flexibility fix with some doggie yoga or suit up in that cute costume and hit the annual Halloween Dog Parade. No matter the season or the size of your canine companion, New York City will leave you and your pooch well rested, rejuvenated and ready for more.

Annual Tompkins Square Halloween Dog Parade

Sit, Stay, See

7th Street to 10th Street between
Avenues A and B, New York,
347-623-3978;
www.firstrunfriends.org

Located in the East Village, the annual Tompkins Square Halloween Dog Parade has garnered a cult following since it's inception in the 1980s and has spawned many similar pageants throughout the city. It is the largest, non-competitive gathering of dog owners in the country, and all proceeds go to the New York City Department of Parks and Recreation. The costumes range from elaborate and fanciful to peculiar and down right strange. Regardless, the event is always entertaining, and many pooches walk away with some substantial prizes for Best in Show, Best Costume, Best Trick and more.

Biscuits & Bath

1535 First Ave., New York, 212-419-2500

Biscuits & Bath Doggie Gym is a dream come true for both busy dog owners and their cage-cranky pets. Boasting a cage-free environment, this 24-hour hound haven is ideal for dogs who don't like being locked up all day. In addition to free roaming, Biscuits and Bath offers a doggy playground, grooming facilities, training programs and walking services. There are six locations throughout the city, and small dog groups are hosted every Monday night.

Canine Court

Van Cortlandt Park, Bronx, 718-430-1890;
www.nycgovparks.org

Forget walks in Central Park. Canine Court, located in the beautiful Van Cortlandt Park in the Bronx, offers so much more for your pooch. As the first public dog playground and agility course in the country, Canine Court offers 14,000 square feet of fenced-in fun for your pet, from hurdles and chutes to teeter-totters and tunnels. Dogs can test their dexterity or simply enjoy a romp with new friends. Either way, they're sure to enjoy themselves and sleep soundly all the way back to the hotel. Dogs must be licensed and vaccinated for rabies.

Canine Cruise

Circle Line Cruises, Pier 83, 42nd Street and Twelfth Avenue, New York, 917-282-4832; *www.caninecruise.com*

There's no better way to see the New York skyline than on a cruise around New York Harbor. Now—finally—your pooch can enjoy the views, too. Currently offered annually, the Canine Cruise welcomes small dogs (under 25 pounds) and their owners for an afternoon of sights, sounds and activities, including a doggie fashion show, canine training tips, caricature drawings and pet photographers. The cost is $40 a person (dogs cruise free!) and all proceeds go to local pet charities.

East Yoga Doga

212 Avenue B, New York, 212-420-8411;
www.eastyoga.com

New York City is known as the city that never sleeps for a reason: it's a stressful environment, even for our four-legged friends. That's why Doga, or dog yoga, has become so popular with New York yogaholics and their dogs alike. East Yoga Doga, a bright and airy studio in the East Village, has taken the trend to heart, offering doga classes weekly to as many as 20 dogs and their owners. From sun salutations to down dog poses, doga affords canines 45 minutes of calming attention and massage. And their owners will get a nice work-out as well. The fee is $17 per class. Schedule varies, see Web site for details.

NYC Pet Fashion Week

125 W. 18th St., New York, 401-331-5073; *www.petfashion-week.com*

Hailed as both a trade show and designer platform, the NYC Pet Fashion Week is a call to animal innovators everywhere. From collars and leashes to foods and fragrances, and of course clothing and accessories, Pet Fashion Week showcases the very best products the industry has to offer your pet. In its first year (2006), the event welcomed 124 exhibitors and nearly 1,500 attendees from all over the world. Whether you're in the market for a new diamond collar for Fifi or simply a more absorbent litter box, the Pet Fashion Week exposition is sure to have what you need (and everything that you don't). The event is held every August. Visit Web site for details.

Prospect Park Dog Beach

Prospect Park Beach, Brooklyn, 718-965-8999;
www.fidobrooklyn.org/features/dogbeach.html

To witness an authentic doggie paddle, head down to Brooklyn where the Prospect Park Dog Beach offers canines an irresistible watering hole. The beach is fenced in to prohibit dogs from swimming too deep, and the park provides a great atmosphere for dogs and owners to mingle with each other. The beach isn't huge, so your pooch may have to wait a bit before taking a dip.

William Secord Gallery

52 E. 76th St., New York, 212-249-3647; *www.dogpainting.com*

If you and your pooch are looking to experience a bit of culture in the Big Apple, head to the William Secord Gallery on Manhattan's Upper East Side. This art haven is all about the dogs, specializing in 19th-century dog paintings, sculptures and drawing. Well-behaved dogs of all sizes are always welcomed guests at the gallery, and treats and bowls of water are provided upon request. Books and souvenirs embracing the history of dogs in art are also available at the gallery. Open Monday through Saturday 10 a.m.-5 p.m. and by appointment; closed Sunday.

Chow Time

Heartland Brewery & Beer Hall ★☆☆☆☆

93 South St., New York, 646-572-2337;
www.heartlandbrewery.com

The Heartland Brewery offers a welcomed respite after an afternoon tour of South Street Seaport. Although it's best known for its classic and seasonal home-brewed beers, the fare is hearty and flavorful, offering everything from smoked brisket chili and cheese grits to mighty red gumbo and collard greens. The outdoor café area welcomes well-behaved pooches with a fresh bowl of water and the occasional doggie treat. You can even score a personalized beer mug to remember the experience by.

American pub menu. Lunch and dinner. Bar. Casual attire. Reservations for inside seating only.

Allegria

66 W. 55th St., New York, 212-956-7755; *www.allegriarestaurant.org*

Although the décor is rather bland, the Italian fare is tasty and well priced at this boite located in Midtown near Central Park, Rockefeller Center and the luxurious shops of Fifth Avenue. The size of the restaurant allows large parties to fit comfortably and keeps wait times to a minimum on busy nights. Quaint outdoor tables offer a nice al fresco experience and remain pet-friendly, with bowls of water provided for parched pooches.

Italian menu. Lunch and dinner. Bar. Business casual attire. Reservations recommended. Outdoor seating.

Amaranth Restaurant

21 E. 62nd St., New York, 212-980-6700; *www.amaranthrestaurant.com*

Draped in crimson and gold, this Upper East Side Mediterranean bistro is an enchanting epicurean treat. The fare is a fusion of French and Italian tastes and offers both small plates and full-sized portions. Service is friendly and approachable, and the menu presents a variety of dishes from a famed foccacia robiola

to steak tartare and homemade ravioli. A charming collection of sidewalk tables allows Amaranth to open its arms to leashed canines as well.

Mediterranean, Italian, French menu. Lunch and dinner. Bar. Business Casual attire. Reservations recommended.

Barking Dog Luncheonette

1453 York Ave., New York, 212-861-3600

From salads and sandwiches to fish and chips and meat loaf, the Barking Dog Luncheonette is a great stop for a family meal. The staff is kid-friendly, and the menu lends itself to picky young appetites. The weekend brunch brings lines that stretch around the corner, so arrive early. A doggy watering fountain outside is only one of many canine amenities at this American cook shack. Leashed dogs are always welcome at the outside tables, and water bowls and tasty treats are on hand.

American, traditional menu. Breakfast, lunch, dinner, weekend brunch. Beer and wine. Casual attire. Reservations not accepted.

Da Rosina Ristorante

342 W. 46th St., New York, 212-977-7373; *www.darosina.com*

For a nice, albeit quick, meal before the curtains go up in the theater district, Da Rosina Ristorante is a good pick. The Italian fare is fresh and straightforward, and the atmosphere echoes the rustic cafés of Italy. Accommodating to couples on dates as well as large groups and bus tours, the restaurant is a good option for tourists looking for a dependable meal. An outside patio makes Da Rosina a pet-friendly restaurant, welcoming dogs of all sizes.

Italian menu. Lunch and dinner. Bar. Casual attire. Reservations recommended.

F & B Gudt Food Restaurant

150 E. 52nd St., New York, 212-421-8600

So, you're in the market for a fast meal, but McDonalds isn't exactly what you had in mind. Head over to F&B, short for Frites and Beignets, which reigns far above the rest when it comes to gourmet fast food. With 22 different hot dogs to choose from and what are often voted the best French fries in Manhattan, F&B is not to be missed. There are two locations—one in the heart of Chelsea and this Midtown delight, which boasts a number of outdoor tables that allow Fido to get in on the fast feast.

Scandinavian, Belgian, German and Austrian menu. Lunch and early dinners. Closed Saturday and Sunday. Beer and wine. Casual attire. Reservations not accepted.

Fred's

476 Amsterdam Ave., New York, 212-579-3076

Fred's, an Upper West Side American staple since the late '90s, is the perfect spot for a quick bite or a relaxing afternoon nosh. The atmosphere is rustic and comfortable with exposed

brick walls and lots of natural light. Although it welcomes young hipsters and families alike, Fred's saves its greatest welcome for man's best friend. Named after a pooch that failed seeing-eye dog school, Fred's is as dog-friendly as they come, with snapshots of canine customers covering the walls and an inviting outdoor café for pets to laze alongside their owners.

American, traditional menu. Lunch, dinner, weekend brunch. Bar. Casual attire. Reservations not accepted.

Grey Dog's Café

33 Carmine St., New York, 212-462-0041; *http://thegreydog. com*

With the familiar aroma of a New England college-town coffee shop, the Grey Dog Café has remained a West Village staple for locals and visitors alike. Bare brick walls and colorful wood tables match the simple menu and partial self-service. The food is reliable and fresh, and the house-blend coffee is strong. People watching is a prime activity at Grey Dog, and local celebs have been known to make an appearance or two. Dogs are allowed at the cafés outdoor tables as well as inside on occasion (with permission).

American café menu. Breakfast, lunch and dinner. Beer and wine. Casual attire. Reservations not accepted. Outdoor seating.

New Leaf Café

1 Margaret Corbin Dr., New York, 212-568-5323;
www.nyrp.org/cafe/

For a more philanthropic dining experience, head up to Manhattan's West Side to the New Leaf Café, an enchanting al fresco dining experience nestled in Fort Tryon Park across from the Cloisters museum. Created by Bette Midler's non-profit group, New York Restoration Project, the New Leaf Café donates all net profit proceeds back to the park and offers a true out-of-Manhattan experience. The seafood-based menu is imaginative and refreshing, and the superb Sunday brunch draws large crowds. The outdoor patio is a perfect spot for pets to enjoy a quiet dog-day afternoon, and the staff is warm and accommodating. Just don't forget your wallet—it's a long way back to the hotel.

American nouveau menu. Lunch and dinner Tuesday and Wednesday; breakfast, lunch and dinner Thursday through Saturday; brunch and dinner Sunday; closed Monday. Bar. Business casual attire. Reservations recommended.

Sidewalk Bar Restaruant

94 Ave. A, New York, 212-473-7373; *www.antifolk.net*

The Sidewalk Bar isn't for the Uptown gourmand—or the hard of hearing. With live music and comedy routines running nightly and a basic menu at best, this Lower East Side haunt is all about the scene. The people watching is eclectic and enter-taining, especially after dark when an alcohol blanket seems to coat the entire street in silliness and farce. Pets are welcomed and revered on the outside patio, but it closes during the winter months, so make sure to bring your pooch when it's still warm outside.

American, traditional menu. Breakfast, lunch and dinner. Bar. Casual attire. Reservations not accepted.

West 79th Street Boat Basin Café

West 79th St., New York, 212-496-5542

It's all about the view at this Upper West Side summer sizzler, located on the banks of the Hudson River. With basic American grilled favorites, the food is simple and the atmosphere is open to all, including four-legged friends (as long as they're leashed). Water bowls and pet treats are dolled out by a friendly waitstaff, and the often large number of dogs makes the experience a social gathering for everyone.

American menu. Lunch, dinner, weekend brunch. Bar. Casual attire. Reservations not accepted.

Zocalo

174 E. 82nd St., New York, 212-717-7772; *www.zocalonyc.com*

Zocalo is the perfect destination to sample sumptuous Mexican cuisine. The interior is colorful and authentic, and traditional folk art lines the walls. Known city-wide for its array of guacamoles, the restaurant presents a modern slant on conventional Mexican fare. The waitstaff are lively and energetic, and the outdoor seating allows for pets of all sizes to get in on the flavor. Dog treats and water bowls are complimentary.

Mexican menu. Dinner Tuesday through Sunday; closed Monday. Bar. Casual attire. Reservations recommended.

Lie Down

Affinia Gardens ★☆☆☆☆

215 E. 64th St., New York, 212-355-1230, 866-246-2203; *www.affinia.com*

Located on the Upper East Side, this all-suite hotel is the perfect choice for a tranquil visit to the Big Apple. The contemporary rooms boast workplaces with ergonomic chairs, kitchens, tranquility kits and pillow menus. The hotel doesn't have an in-house restaurant, but four restaurants in the immediate vicinity provide room service—one offers 24-hour service. A special Jet Set Pet program offers welcome walks, day care, grooming services, and gourmet cakes and cookies for special occasions. A pet psychic is also available upon request.

130 rooms, all suites. High-speed, wireless Internet access. Fitness room. Airport transportation available. Business center. $$$

Algonquin Hotel ★★☆☆☆

59 W. 44th St., New York, 212-840-6800; 888-304-2047;
www.algonquinhotel.com

Originally opened in 1902, this hotel in the heart of Midtown became famous as a gathering spot for writers and theatrical performers. The legendary Algonquin Round Table, which formed after World War I, included such illustrious writers as Dorothy Parker and George S. Kaufman. Additional regulars included Booth Tarkington, H. L. Mencken and Gertrude Stein. That spirit lives on in the Oak Room, the Algonquin's supper club, where guests can catch well-known cabaret acts on Tuesday through Saturday evenings. Because of the famed Algonquin cat-in-residence, Matilda, the hotel only accepts dogs under 10 pounds, charging a $75 fee per night.

174 rooms. High-speed, wireless Internet access. Two restaurants, bar. Fitness room. Airport transportation available. $$$

City Club Hotel ★★★☆☆

55 W. 44th St., New York, 212-921-5500, 877-367-2269;
www.cityclubhotel.com

A world away from its former life as a gentlemen's club, the City Club Hotel is all about contemporary style and elegance. From the Frette bed linens to the Hermes bath products, this intimate boutique hotel spoils its guests with luxurious amenities, not to mention attentive service. With Times Square and Fifth Avenue shopping only a block away, you won't have to go far to explore some of New York's most famous spots. And if you're looking for one of New York's best meals, you won't even have to leave the hotel; world-renowned chef Daniel Boulud's acclaimed DB Bistro Moderne is adjacent to the hotel lobby. Though pets aren't invited to nosh on the famed

DB burger, they are welcome in the hotel with a $100 deposit (which is returned at checkout as long as Sparky doesn't chew off a leg of the nightstand).

65 rooms. High-speed Internet access. Restaurant, bar. $$

Four Seasons Hotel New York ★★★★★

57 E. 57th St., New York, 212-758-5700, 800-819-5053; *www.fourseasons.com*

The busy world of 57th Street's designer boutiques and office towers awaits outside the doors of the Four Seasons Hotel New York, which was designed by legendary architect I. M. Pei. The rooms and suites are testaments to chic simplicity with neutral tones, English sycamore furnishings, and state-of-the-art technology, but it's the service that defines the Four Seasons experience. The staff makes guests feel completely at ease in the monumental building. Pets are pampered at the Four Seasons as well, as long as they weigh less than 15 pounds. Special pet beds and bowls are provided upon check-in, and walking services are available through the hotel's pages.

370 rooms. High-speed, wireless Internet access. Restaurant, bar. Fitness room, spa. Airport transportation available. Business center. $$$$

Hampton Inn Manhattan Chelsea ★☆☆☆☆

108 W. 24th St., New York, 212-414-1000, 800-426-7866; *www.hamptoninn.com*

Located in trendy Chelsea, which borders the West Village and Midtown Manhattan, this hotel offers the best of both worlds—an affordable, family-friendly hotel near the bustle of the city. A full breakfast is included in the room rate—an extra savings for families. Another family-friendly perk: the family pet gets to come along, as long as he weighs in at less than 25 pounds. A $25 fee will be charged for each four-legged companion.

144 rooms. Complimentary full breakfast. Fitness room. $$

Holiday Inn Express New York City Fifth Avenue ★☆☆☆☆

15 W. 45th St., New York, 212-302-9088; 800-315-2621; *www.holidayinnexpress.com*

This Holiday Inn Express, located just west of Fifth Avenue, is near Times Square and its theaters, restaurants, and shops. The simple, no-nonsense hotel is suitable for business travelers, tourists, or those traveling with families. Pets are always welcome, for a fee of $50 per pet, and a booklet is provided outlining convenient pet-friendly services, including restaurants, grooming centers and dog parks.

125 rooms. Complimentary continental breakfast. High-speed, wireless Internet access. Airport transportation available. Business center. $$$

Hotel Plaza Athénée ★★★☆☆

37 E. 64th St., New York, 212-734-9100, 800-447-8800; *www. plaza-athenee.com*

Hotel Plaza Athénée is the perfect place to enjoy a little bit of France while visiting New York City. Located between Park and Madison Avenues in one of the city's most exclusive neighborhoods—the Upper East Side—this elegant hotel has a decidedly residential feel. A palette of blues, golds, and reds marks the French contemporary design of the rooms and suites. Some suites have dining rooms, while others have indoor terraces or outdoor balconies. Through the hotel's special pet-friendly program, animals weighing less than 25 pounds can check in for a fee of $60. Dog beds, treats and water bowls are provided upon arrival to make pets feel right at home.

149 rooms. High-speed, wireless Internet access. Restaurant, bar. Fitness room. Airport transportation available. Business center. $$$$

Mandarin Oriental, New York ★★★★★

80 Columbus Circle, New York, 212-805-8800, 866-801-8880;
www.mandarinoriental.com/newyork/

One look through a window in the Mandarin Oriental, New York, could spoil guests for other New York City hotels forever. Part of the Time Warner Center, the first floor of the hotel sits high above the city on the 35th floor of the building (the hotel continues up to the 54th floor). Views of Central Park, the Hudson River, and the city skyline provide a dazzling backdrop to a luxurious experience. Though luxurious guest rooms make it tempting to laze about for hours on end, slip out to explore all that the hotel and the Time Warner Center have to offer. Want to be dazzled by one of the world's best chefs? Call ahead to make reservations at one of the much-talked-about restaurants near the hotel, including Thomas Keller's Per Se and Masa Takayama's Masa. Pets are always a welcomed addition at the Mandarin Oriental. Dog beds, food and toys are provided upon check-in. Walking services can be arranged through the concierge.

248 rooms. Pets accepted. High-speed, wireless Internet access. Two restaurants, bar. Fitness room, fitness classes available, spa. Indoor pool, whirlpool. Business center. $$$$

The Mansfield ★★☆☆☆

12 W. 44th St., New York, 212-277-8700, 800-255-5167; *www.mansfieldhotel.com*

Upon entering this Midtown hotel, you'll feel as if you've been transported back in time to the early 1900s. The club-like surroundings include dark woods and original terrazzo floors in the lobby. The stylish guest rooms feature ebony-stained hardwood floors, 300-count linens with down comforters, and pillow-top mattresses, black-and-white photographs, chrome accent lighting, and CD players. The luxurious bathrooms feature black Cambrian marble baths, plush cotton robes, and Aveda bath products. The M Bar, with its domed skylight, Beaux Arts lighting, and comfortable lounge seating, is the perfect spot for evening cocktails. The Mansfield welcomes all pets weighing less than 25 pounds.

126 rooms. Complimentary continental breakfast. High-speed,

wireless Internet access. Restaurant, bar. Fitness room. Airport transportation available. Business center. $$

The Mercer ★★★☆☆

147 Mercer St., New York, 212-966-6060; *www.mercerhotel.com*

Catering to a fashion-forward clientele in New York's SoHo, the Mercer Hotel is a boutique hotel set in the midst of one of the city's most exciting neighborhoods. Christian Liaigre, darling of the minimalist design movement, created a sophisticated look for the hotel with simple furnishings and serene neutral colors. The uncluttered scheme extends to the bathrooms, which have clean white tiles and luxurious two-person bathtubs or spacious showers with assorted spray fixtures. The lobby has a lending library stocked with popular books and videos, and the nearby trend-setting Crunch Gym is accessible to all guests. Mercer Kitchen and Bar reign as hotspots for both their sensational food (under the direction of celeb chef Jean-Georges Vongerichten) and their fabulous people watching. The Mercer Hotel is very pet-friendly, inviting animals of all sizes (except horses, of course), and offers walking services through the bellman.

75 rooms. High-speed, wireless Internet access. Restaurant, bar. Business center. $$$$

The Muse ★★★☆☆

130 W. 46th St., New York, 212-485-2400; 800-546-7866; *www.themusehotel.com*

A designer's dream, this hotel's unique restored triple-arched, limestone- and brick-façade gives it a dramatic feel. Original artwork celebrating the theater and the performing arts hangs in each room, which are decorated in a warm color scheme of rust, burgundy, pear green, and muted blue with cherry wood furniture. Custom linens and duvet-covered feather beds add to the comfort level. Baths are green marble with stone vanities and upgraded bath products. Other distinguishing features include in-room spa services, balconies, and DVD players. Pets of all sizes are also treated well. They're given special beds and snacks, and the hotel will arrange sitting services if needed. Owners must provide recent vet certificates and proof that their pets are on flea medication on check-in.

200 rooms. High-speed Internet access. Restaurant, bar. Fitness room. Airport transportation available. $$$

The Ritz-Carlton New York Battery Park
★★★★☆

2 West St., New York, 212-344-0800; 800-542-8680; *www.ritzcarlton.com*

While only a five-minute walk from Wall Street and the Financial District, the Ritz-Carlton feels light-years away with the views of the Hudson River, the Statue of Liberty, and Ellis Island from its location on the southern tip of Manhattan. This 38-story glass-and-brick tower is a departure from the traditional Ritz-Carlton European style, from the contemporary glass artwork to the modern furnishings in rooms and suites.

The service is distinctly Ritz-Carlton, however, with exceptional concierge service and even bath butlers who create special concoctions for bath time. The experience is no less lavish for the hotel's four-legged guests, as long as they weigh less than 20 pounds. There is a $125 fee for pets, but the concierge can arrange everything from walking services to grooming spa appointments.

298 rooms. High-speed, wireless Internet access. Restaurant, two bars. Fitness room, spa. Business center. $$$$

Soho Grand Hotel ★★★☆☆

310 W. Broadway, New York, 212-965-3000, 800-965-3000; *www.sohogrand.com*

Calculated cool is the best way to describe this trendy downtown hotel. Guest rooms are simple in design, with tones of black and white and clean, uncluttered baths. All rooms have stereos, and some have rocking chairs. The Grand Bar & Lounge serves a mix of dishes, from macaroni and cheese to lobster tea sandwiches and chickpea-fried rock shrimp. The lounge also features music and DJs, making it a good place to hang out

pampering services for pets (using products made with botanical ingredients) as well as accessories for the fashionable dog.

Rittenhouse Square

Walnut Street, Rittenhouse Square Street and 18th Street, Philadelphia; *www.ushistory.org/districts/rittenhouse/*

The chic and upper-crust Rittenhouse Square is surrounded by some of Philadelphia's most exclusive apartment buildings and shops. The urban square, filled with park benches and green space, is one of the places to be seen on a sunny afternoon, and many people bring their four-legged companions.

Schuylkill River Dog Park

25th St. between Pine and Locust, Philadelphia

This well-maintained fenced dog run is located across the Schuylkill River from Philadelphia's famous 30th Street Station and is probably the center of the city's dog community. There's a section for smaller dogs and one for their larger brethren. The run is part of the larger Schuylkill River Park, which has riverfront trails, playgrounds and gardens.

Valley Forge National Historical Park

Valley Forge, 24 miles northwest on I-76, 610-783-1077;

www.nps.gov/vafo/

George Washington and his men spent a harsh winter at what is now a 3,500-acre park just outside Philadelphia. Accessible via the Schuylkill River Trail (about 20 miles), the park has trails and walking paths that are open to pets. There are even popular horse trails. Cabins, replicas of the ones where Washington's troops lived, are scattered throughout the park, as are various monuments, cannons and even some archeological sites. Pets, though welcome during the day, are not permitted to stay the night at the campsite.

Chow Time

White Dog Café ★★☆☆☆

3420 Sansom St., Philadelphia, 215-386-9224 ;
www.whitedog.com

White Dog Café is situated in the former house of author Madame Blavatsky, founder of the Theosophical Society. The furnishings are primarily antiques, and there is a strong canine theme throughout as well as a touch of Victorian decor. A local favorite, this family-friendly eatery offers a varied and interesting menu, which includes American and vegetarian dishes using local and organic ingredients. There are a few outdoor tables on the front terrace where you can dine with your dog.

American, vegetarian menu. Lunch, dinner, brunch. Bar. Children's menu. Business casual attire. Reservations recommended. Outdoor seating.

Also Recommended

Deuce Restaurant and Bar

40 N. Second St., Philadelphia, 215-413-3822;
www.deucerestaurant.com

98 rooms. High-speed Internet access. Four restaurants, two bars. Fitness room, fitness classes available, spa. Indoor pool. Business center. $$$$

★★★☆☆The Ritz-Carlton, Philadelphia

10 Avenue of the Arts, Philadelphia, 215-523-8000, 800-542-8680; *www.ritzcarlton.com*

This hotel breathes new life into a magnificent historic building in the center of Philadelphia's downtown business district. This one-time home to Girard and Mellon Banks, designed in the 1900s by the architectural firm of McKim, Mead, and White, was inspired by Rome's Pantheon. Marrying historic significance with trademark Ritz-Carlton style, this Philadelphia showpiece boasts handsome and striking decor. The rooms and

suites are luxurious, and Club Level accommodations include access to a private lounge filled with food and drink. The hotel offers a pillow menu, a bath butler, and other unique services. Dining options are plentiful, and the Sunday jazz brunch is a local favorite. Animals of any size can stay for a $75 fee with advance notice of their arrival. A waiver must be signed, and while on the premises, pets must be accompanied by their owners at all times.

300 rooms. High-speed, wireless Internet access. Two restaurants, two bars. Fitness room, spa. Airport transportation available. Business center. $$$

Sheraton Society Hill ★★★☆☆

1 Dock St., Philadelphia, 215-238-6000, 800-325-3535;
www.sheraton.com/societyhill/

This Sheraton is located in the Society Hill historic district and within walking distance of historical sites. A brick building on a cobblestone street, the hotel features colonial decor, exposed brick walls in the lobby area, and an atrium. Dogs weighing less than 80 pounds can stay at no extra charge. The property offers a Suite Sleeper dog bed and is located close to walking paths along the Delaware River. 365 rooms. High-speed, wireless Internet access. Two restaurants, two bars. Fitness room. Indoor pool, children's pool, whirlpool. Business center. $$

Sheraton University City ★★★☆☆

36th and Chestnut Streets, Philadelphia, 215-387-8000,
800-325-3535;
www.philadelphiasheraton.com

Perfect for visitors to the University of Pennsylvania, this Sheraton is located in the midst of an eclectic university environment. The hotel's early American decor and lobby fireplace give it a cozy feel, and the friendly staff makes a stay here even more pleasant. Dogs up to 80 pounds are accepted; bowls and beds are available on request.

316 rooms. High-speed Internet access. Restaurant, bar. Fitness room. Outdoor pool. Business center. $$

Sofitel Philadelphia ★★★☆☆

120 S. 17th St., Philadelphia, 215-569-8300, 800-763-4835; *www.sofitel.com*

Modern French style permeates the Sofitel Philadelphia. This elegant hotel sits on the former site of the Philadelphia Stock Exchange, and its downtown Center City location makes it ideal for both business and leisure travelers. The rooms and suites are exceedingly stylish, with plush beds and contemporary furniture. The lobby bar, La Bourse, is comfortable and chic, while the bistro fare and unique setting of Chez Colette recall the romance of 1920s Paris. Up to two dogs or cats can stay with their owners for free.

306 rooms. High-speed, wireless Internet access. Restaurant, bar. Fitness room. Business center. $$$

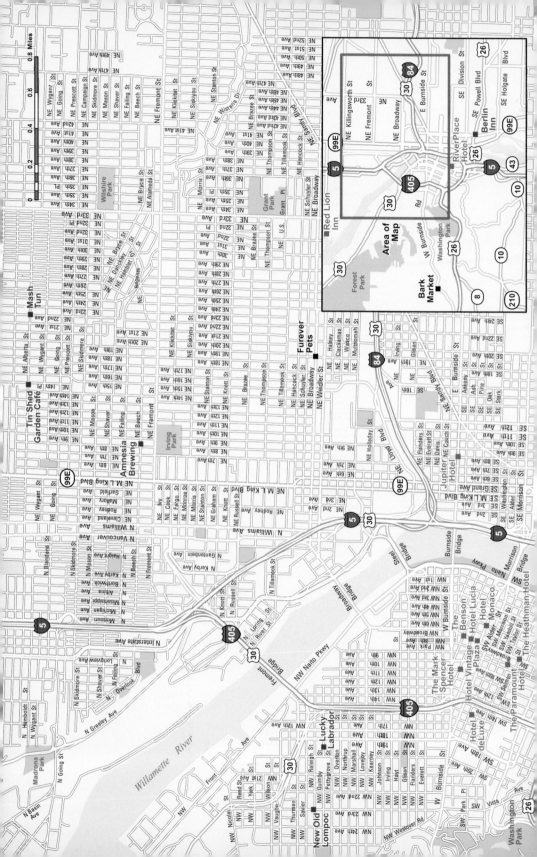

In some cities, "dog-friendly" might mean "sure, you can bring your mutt in here if you plunk down some serious cash, keep a muzzle on the guy, never let us see or hear the thing, and enter through the back door." Not in Portland. Here, even the nicest hotels put all paws on deck to give a warm welcome. Dogs are ushered through the front door with welcome signs announcing their furry presence, and after enjoying their free treats, they can even nose through their own doggie room service menu (sometimes from the luxury of a Temper-Pedic bed!)

Bark Market

460-B W. Miller Rd., Portland, 503-914-5944; *www.thebarkmarket.com*

Help your pet join Portland's organic food movement with a chew or kibble from this holistic pet store, where all the food and products are organic and healthy. Toys range from the famous Chuck-It ball launcher to organic catnip-filled plush chipmunks and turtles.

The Great Outdoors

One reason Portland and pets go hand-in-paw: It's an outdoorsy city, and have you ever met a mutt who doesn't relish the great outdoors? And when you're ready to sightsee in the city, you're still covered—store owners in Portland are notoriously dog-friendly. They have been known, when seeing you tie your dog up outside, to let you know that you can bring your pooch in, or they will run out with treats if you decide to shop solo inside. Don't be surprised if you strike up a few conversations while walking your dog on the streets, too; Portland is a friendly city, and dogs often serve as ice-breakers. If you want room to roam, there are 31 official off-leash dog parks scattered throughout the various city neighborhoods; for an official listing, go to the Portland Parks and Recreation Web site at *www.portlandonline.com/parks*.

Furever Pets

1902 E. Broadway St. Portland, 503-282-4225

This popular pet store stocks little luxuries for furry friends, from rhinestone collars to posh rain slickers, perfect for Portland's rainy weather. The friendly staff can also offer tips on pet nutrition or special order hard to find gear and pet clothes.

Chow Time

It's hard to offer a comprehensive listing of dog-friendly restaurants in Portland. Essentially anywhere there is outdoor seating, dogs are allowed, and Portland, being an outdoorsy city, has plenty of outdoor areas at its restaurants. Since Portland is also the unofficial brewery capital of the nation, it's only natural that most of the restaurants listed are also microbreweries, which often have outdoors patios and staffs that are especially happy to see a furry face. These are the best of the bunch and often offer a dog theme, an especially generous or dog-friendly outdoors area, and sometimes even a special pet menu.

Also Recommended

Amnesia Brewing

832 N. Beech St., Portland, 503-281-7708

In Portland, it seems that every neighborhood has its own brewpub, and the funky Mississippi area is no exception. The Amnesia brewpub, located in a converted warehouse, has an enormous covered front outdoors area filled with picnic tables, which are great for people watching. The beers are popular, and the menu, while limited, will make you feel as though you're at a friend's barbecue, with spicy sausage and burgers grilled right on the patio.

Barbecue menu. Dinner. Casual attire.

Berlin Inn

3131 E. 12th and Powell Blvd., Portland, 503-236-6761; *www.berlininn.com*

You don't need to have a German shepherd to enjoy the Berlin Inn—all breeds will want to lap up the special doggie menu at this authentic German restaurant. Wash down your Wiener schnitzel with a large selection of German-style beers and wines.

German menu. Breakfast, lunch, dinner. Casual attire.

Lucky Labrador Beer Hall

1945 W. Quimby St., Portland, 503-517-4352; *www.luckylab.com*

The newest kid to join the Lucky Lab family (there are two other locations) is right in the industrial area of the popular Northwest neighborhood, housed in a cavernous trucking warehouse. Dog-themed artwork hangs on the walls, pictures of canine customers are pinned to the bulletin board, and paws are allowed in the outdoor seating area. The menu includes the popular bento dishes and a wide variety of sandwiches, including made-to-order creations.

American menu. Lunch, dinner. Casual attire.

Mash Tun

2204 E. Alberta St., Portland, 503-548-4491

Another small brewpub with a neighborhood feel has moved into the up-and-coming Alberta neighborhood. Friendly bartenders, a free jukebox, a covered outdoors patio where dogs are made to feel welcome, and beers brewed onsite add to standard pub menu offerings.

Pub menu. Lunch and dinner on weekends, dinner only during the week. Casual attire.

New Old Lompoc

1616 W. 23rd Ave., Portland, 503-225-1855;
www.newoldlompoc.com

The huge back outdoor deck makes this place a hit on summer weekends, and the handcrafted beer makes it popular year-round. Friendly bartenders give New Old Lompoc a neighborhood feel, and the large sandwich and salad selection will fill you up. We like it because it's conveniently located right in the popular Northwest neighborhood, yet it never has that too-busy feel.

American menu. Lunch, dinner. Bar. Casual attire.

Tin Shed Garden Café

1438 E. Alberta St., Portland, 503-288-6966;
www.tinshedgardencafe.com

The outdoors area at the Tin Shed makes you feel as though you're in someone's personal sanctuary, and sometimes you'll feel outnumbered if you don't have a dog along. An inventive, varied and vegetarian-friendly menu includes sandwiches, pastas, burgers, and the famous breakfasts, plus one of the best happy hours in town. A special dog menu includes Hambarker Helper (rice, garlic, mushrooms and garden burger) and Kibbles 'N Bacon Bits (rice, garlic, mushrooms, free-range hamburger and bacon bits).

American menu. Breakfast, lunch, dinner. Closed Monday evenings. Bar. Casual attire.

The Benson Hotel★★★☆☆

309 W. Broadway, Portland, 503-228-2000, 888-523-6766;
www.bensonhotel.com

This historic hotel, built in 1912, is stately and opulent. Every president since Truman has stayed in the VIP suite. The spacious lobby alone is worth a visit—have a drink next to the piano bar. Pets also get the presidential treatment here—for $75 per stay, the "Benson Buddies" program includes a Temper-Pedic memory foam doggie bed (don't be jealous, humans also get them), take-home treat package, a pet-friendly area guide, and food and water bowls.

287 rooms. High-speed, wireless Internet access. Restaurant, bar. Fitness room. Business center. $$

The Heathman Hotel ★★★☆☆

1001 W. Broadway, Portland, 503-241-4100, 800-551-0011;
www.heathmanhotel.com

At the historic and elegant Heathman Hotel, you can actually choose from three different bed types—soft, medium, and firm. That's one of many personalized touches that makes this grand hotel in downtown Portland stand apart. From an Andy Warhol silkscreen to mirrors from the Waldorf Astoria hotel, the 250-piece art collection is worth a trip itself. The literary arts aren't left out, either—more than 3,000 signed editions of classics from famous guests, including Tom Wolfe, John Updike, and Joyce Carol Oates, make up the permanent library collection. Pets aren't left out of the picture, either—for a $35 fee per night, your companion can soak in the glamorous atmosphere.

150 rooms. High-speed Internet access. Restaurant, bar. Fitness room. Business center. $$

Hotel Lucia★★★☆☆

400 S.W. Broadway, Portland, 503-225-1717, 877-225-1717;
www.hotellucia.com

Hotel Lucia opened in 2002 and achieved instant fame for its trendy style, tasty room service from Typhoon! Thai restaurant, and small cozy rooms with super-comfortable beds. Photos from Pulitzer prize-winning (and Oregon native) David Hume Kennerly line the walls and add to the minimal, modern décor. A $35 fee will score your furry friend a bed, food bowls, treats and toys.

128 rooms. High-speed, wireless Internet access. Restaurant, bar. $$

Hotel Monaco ★★★☆☆

506 W. Washington St., Portland,

503-222-0001, 888-207-2201;
www.monaco-portland.com

Formerly known as the 5th Avenue Suites, the Hotel Monaco was transformed in February 2007 into the glorious hostelry that it is today. As with all Kimpton hotels, there's a theme: patron of the arts. Local artists get their own gallery, and you

can try out your mad artist skills at the nightly wine hour. The historic hotel dates back to 1912, when it housed the Lipman Wolf department store. A yellow lab named Art (the staff call him the director of public relations) greets guests checking into the Monaco. Your pet will get a special shout-out on the lobby welcome board, and treats include a dog bed and water bowl, pet psychic and masseuse (extra charges apply), and a free stay for pets of any size.

221 rooms. High-speed, wireless Internet access. Restaurant, bar. Fitness room. On-site Aveda spa. Business center. $$

Hotel Vintage Plaza ★★★☆☆

422 S.W. Broadway, Portland, 503-228-1212, 800-263-2305; *www.vintageplaza.com*

This elegant Kimpton hotel's name is appropriate—the hotel is housed in a historic building that was constructed in 1894 as the Imperial Hotel, and it is listed on the National Register of Historic Places. It's also aptly named because of its dedication to wine: The rooms are named after local wineries, and a nightly wine hour will get you acquainted with the area's grapes (Oregon's Willamette Valley is quickly becoming known as the next Napa). The rooms aren't your standard bed-and-bathroom

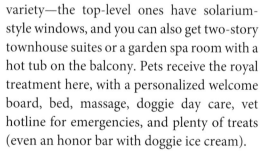

variety—the top-level ones have solarium-style windows, and you can also get two-story townhouse suites or a garden spa room with a hot tub on the balcony. Pets receive the royal treatment here, with a personalized welcome board, bed, massage, doggie day care, vet hotline for emergencies, and plenty of treats (even an honor bar with doggie ice cream).

107 rooms. High-speed, wireless Internet access. Restaurant, bar. Fitness room. In-room spa services. Business center. $$

Paramount Hotel ★★★☆☆

808 W. Taylor St., Portland, 503-223-9900; *www.portlandparamount.com*

Unlike most of the downtown hotels, which

costs just $8 to wash any size dog, and best of all, the friendly staff will clean up after you.

Lucky Dog Pet Boutique

415 Market St., San Diego, 619-696-0364;
www.shopluckydog.com

Since August 2002, Lucky Dog has offered distinctive pet products for discriminating canines and their owners. The Market Street boutique, located in the Gaslamp Quarter, features a dog bar and nutrition center complete with healthy treats. A Lucky Dog photo gallery shows off the store's frequent customers. The shelves are stocked with couture clothing, beautiful bedding, fun toys and accessories.

Muttropolis

7755 Girard Ave., La Jolla, 858-459-9663;
www.muttropolis.com

Treat your dog and cat to the best San Diego has to offer at Muttropolis, an upscale pet supply boutique. Here you'll find high-fashion collars, fish tanks, and costumes along with everything needed for food, bowls, grooming and toys. Beat kitty blahs and the doggie downs with innovative toys. Home decor goes to the dogs with designer pet beds crafted from fashionable fabrics. The store has a doggy TV lounge where pets can check out videos. Pooch parties, mutt mingles, and book signings also take place regularly.

Petco Park

100 Park Blvd., San Diego, 619-795-5000;
http://sandiego.padres.mlb.com

A trip to San Diego in the summer wouldn't be complete without taking in a Padre's baseball game at Petco Park, named after the San Diego-based pet supplies retailer that paid for naming rights. Once a year, the Padres open Petco to canines who want to take in a game with their owners. Dogs parade before the game and sit in a special section of the

park to watch the competition with their owners. Throughout the year, there is an open 2.5-acre park beyond the center field fence with a panoramic view of the field, which lets owners and their pets take in the scene on off-game days.

Chow Time

Sally's Seafood on the Water ★★★☆☆

1 Market Place, San Diego, 619-358-6740;
http://sallyssandiego.com

Although located on the Boardwalk adjacent to the Manchester Grand Hyatt, this is no tourist trap. Lots of locals come here to enjoy the beautiful waterfront views and ultra-fresh seafood, which includes pan-fried diver scallops with lychee relish, and ahi tuna with miso-mustard. The crab cakes, which are likely grilled (not fried), are also said to be some of the best in the city. Well-behaved, leashed dogs are allowed on the terrace.

American menu. Breakfast, lunch, dinner. Bar. Casual attire. Reservations recommended. Valet parking. Outdoor seating. $$$

Also Recommended

The Dancing Dog Deli

1501 India St. #105, San Diego, 619-230-1222

Although there's no dancing dog on staff, your pet might dance for treats at this establishment while you munch on sandwiches. This small deli, located in Little Italy, also offers meals to go for both you and your pet.

Deli menu. Breakfast, lunch, dinner.

Korky's Ice Cream and Coffee

2371 San Diego Ave., San Diego, 619-297-3080

Indulge in some old-fashioned ice cream or Italian gelato at this laid-back café in Old Town. The neighborhood coffee house makes custom coffees and milkshakes and also offers light fare of sandwiches, salads and pastries. Pets are welcome at the outside tables.

American menu. Breakfast, lunch, dinner.

Moondoggie's

832 Garnet Ave., Pacific Beach, 858-483-6550;
www.moondoggies.com

A local favorite, this sports bar and grill is known for its casual southern California fare, such as chicken tequila lime pasta, and lobster tacos. There are also plenty of canine-inspired drinks— the Dogarita, Berry Bad Dog and the K-9 Kosmo. Dogs and their owners can relax on the large outdoor patio, which has heated lamps for cooler months.

American menu. Lunch, dinner. Bar.

Terra

1270 Cleveland Ave., Pacific Beach, 619-293-7088,
www.terrasd.com

This upscale bistro has ample patio space for al fresco dining with your favorite furry friend. The restaurant provides a puppy menu with delicacies such as puppy pizzas and pig's ears.

American menu. Lunch, dinner, brunch. Bar.

Zia's Bistro

1845 India St., San Diego, 619-234-1344; *www.ziasbistro.com*

At Zia's, happiness means food, friendship, and a glass of wine. The northernmost patio has a view of San Diego Bay, and dogs are welcome outside.

Although the restaurant doesn't have a traditional kids' menu, the staff will customize dishes for younger taste buds.

Italian. Breakfast, lunch, dinner.

Lie Down

Bristol Hotel ★★★☆☆

1055 First Ave., San Diego, 619-232-6141; 800-662-4477; *www.thebristolsandiego.com*

This downtown boutique hotel lures young professionals and couples with its funky, contemporary vibe. A pop art collection includes works by Andy Warhol, Roy Lichtenstein, and Keith Haring. Rooms are decorated with bold colors and include free Internet access, salon-style hair dryers, honor bars and CD players. The top-floor ballroom features a retractable roof, and the bistro is a favorite among locals who come here for the signature drink, the Craizi Daizi martini. Pets under 50 pounds are accepted with a $50 fee. Dogs must be on a leash when in the lobby and cannot be left unattended in the room. Book in advance because dogs are only allowed in third-floor rooms.

102 rooms. Restaurant, bar. Fitness room. $$

Doubletree Hotel Mission Valley ★★★☆☆

7450 Hazard Center Dr., San Diego, 619-297-5466, 800-222-8733; *www.doubletree.com*

This comfortable hotel is close to many major attractions, including SeaWorld and the San Diego Zoo, and

West Inn & Suites

4970 Avendia Encitas, Carlsbad, 866-431-9378;
www.westinnandsuites.com

This boutique hotel is just a short drive from the South Carlsbad beach, Carlsbad Premium Outlets, and Legoland California. The smoke-free property features king-size, pillow-top beds, complimentary breakfast, a free shuttle around Carlsbad and two restaurants. Fresh flowers and bottled water can be found in each room. The hotel is pet-friendly and charges $75 for one night or a $150 flat fee for two nights or more. Pets and their families are greeted with their names written on a chalkboard at the front desk.

86 rooms. Two restaurants. High-speed Internet access. $$

Woodfin Suites

10044 Pacific Mesa Blvd., San Diego, 858-597-0500,
888-433-2150; *www.woodfinsuitehotels.com*

Spacious suites offer fully equipped kitchens, separate living and dining areas, cable TV including HBO, DVD player, comfortable beds, and workspace areas with high-speed Internet access. The Oasis Bar & Grill features a bamboo and mahogany bar, and a tropical poolside patio provides plenty of plush seating. There is an onsite pantry, laundry facilities, and DVD movie library. This hotel welcomes pets of any size for a $10 charge.

194 rooms. Restaurant. Fitness center. $$

San Francisco Bay

San Fran Maritime Natl. Hist. Park

Golden Gate N.R.A.

George R. Moscone Recreation Center

Russian Hill Park

Washington Square Park

Pioneer Park

Lafayette Square Park

Alta Plaza Park

Jefferson Square Park

Hayward Playground

Civic Center

Union Square

Waterfront

The Embarcadero

Restaurants & Hotels
Hotel Vitale
Chaya
Harbor Court Hotel
Fog City Diner
Globe
Figaro
Rose Pistola
Omni Hotel
The Ritz-Carlton, San Francisco
Palace Hotel
W San Francisco
Campton Place Hotel
Four Seasons Hotel San Francisco
Hotel Monaco
Wags Pet Wash & Boutique
Bella & Daisy's
Perry's
Betelnut Pejiu Wu
PlumpJack Balboa Cafe
Rose's Cafe
Baker Street Bistro
Paragon

Streets
King St
Bryant St
Brannan St
Delancey St
Harrison St
Folsom St
Howard St
Mission St
Minna St
Jessie St
Market St
1st St
2nd St
3rd St
4th St
5th St
6th St
Steuart St
Spear St
Main St
Beale St
Fremont St
Drumm St
Davis St
Front St
Battery St
Sansome St
Montgomery St
Kearny St
Grant Ave
Stockton St
Powell St
Mason St
Taylor St
Jones St
Leavenworth St
Hyde St
Larkin St
Polk St
Van Ness Ave
Franklin St
Gough St
Octavia St
Laguna St
Buchanan St
Webster St
Fillmore St
Steiner St
Pierce St
Scott St
Divisadero St
Broderick St
Baker St
Lyon St
California St
Sacramento St
Clay St
Washington St
Jackson St
Pacific Ave
Broadway
Vallejo St
Green St
Union St
Filbert St
Greenwich St
Lombard St
Chestnut St
Francisco St
Bay St
North Point St
Beach St
Jefferson St
Marina Blvd
Yacht Rd
Avila St
Cervantes Blvd
Retiro Way
Marina Green Dr
Columbus Ave
Sutter St
Post St
Geary St
Geary Blvd
O'Farrell St
Ellis St
Eddy St
Turk St
Golden Gate Ave
McAllister St
Maiden Ln

Pine St
Bush St
Sansome St
Battery St
Sacramento St

0 0.1 0.2 0.4 0.6 0.8 Miles

Area of Map (inset)
Pacific Ocean
Universal Cafe
Babies
Zuni Cafe
San Francisco Inn
Buena Vista Park
Fort Funston
80
280
101
35
1

San Francisco

Few cities in the United States can claim to have a higher population of pooches than children, but San Francisco is proudly one of them. (The local dog population is estimated at around 120,000, while there are fewer than 113,000 kids.) And that surely explains why the City by the Bay boasts an ever-increasing number of establishments boasting pet-friendly policies. With swank hotels, gourmet eateries and stores now catering to canines, it's safe to say that dogs have the run of the town.

Mild weather most days of the year means you and your four-legged friends can enjoy the city on foot. When it's time for play, San Francisco hosts the spacious Golden Gate Park and numerous neighborhood green spaces every few blocks, all with designated off-leash areas. Nights can be cool when the fog rolls in, but the plethora of pet boutiques are well stocked with items like rain slickers and hand-knit sweaters to ward off the chill.

Alta Plaza Park

Sit, Stay, See

Scott, Clay, Jackson and Steiner Streets, San Francisco

Another park with a view, Alta Plaza sits on a hill in the Pacific Heights neighborhood. If you're a pug owner and happen to be in the city on the first Sunday of the month, don't miss "Pug Day" at the park, an informal gathering of pooches and their

proud parents starting anytime after 2 p.m.

Babies

235 Gough St., San Francisco, 415-701-7387, 888-701-7386; *www.babiessf.com*

If your dog's wardrobe rivals your own, Babies is the place to stock up on outfits for fashion-forward canines. Here you'll find ballerina dresses, hoodies, houndstooth raincoats and more, plus a large selection of beds, collars and treats.

Bella & Daisy's

1750 Union St., San Francisco, 415-440-7007; *www.bellaanddaisys.com*

The high-end dog carriers and couture fashions are impressive, but go to Bella & Daisy's for its gourmet treats. The bakery offers everything from made-to-order birthday cakes to doggie cannoli and pizza.

Buena Vista Park

Haight Street and Buena Vista Avenue, San Francisco

This park is the city's oldest and one of the most amenable to dogs. No leash is required. On top of the woody hills is a great lookout point with views of the East Bay and the Golden Gate Bridge.

Fort Funston

Route 35 (Skyline Blvd.), San Francisco;

www.fortfunstondog.org

If you'd rather make a whole day of the park, pack a picnic and head to Fort Funston, which is south of the San Francisco Zoo. This canine retreat boasts dune trails, beach access and plenty of room to roam around and socialize.

Wags Pet Wash & Boutique

1840 Polk St., 415-409-2472; *www.sfwags.com*

Wags offers professional grooming, puppy day care and DIY dog washing that is perfect for out-of-town visitors. The store provides blow dryers, towels and your choice of organic shampoos. Or opt for the full service, which includes a nail trimming and finishing conditioning spritz.

Baker Street Bistro ★☆☆☆☆

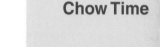

Chow Time

2953 Baker St., San Francisco, 415-931-1475

Near the Presidio in Cow Hollow, this tiny but popular neighborhood French bistro draws customers from all over the city. With only about 15 tables and basic furnishings and decor, the restaurant relies on its excellent bang-for-the-buck factor. A small open kitchen is located at the rear of one room, while a service bar is at the rear of the other. Banquettes run along the walls, and small tables are set with a white tablecloth topped

with glass. The menu, which changes daily, comprises a handful of entrees and a solid wine list. A collection of local artwork is available for sale. Dogs are welcome guests at the sidewalk tables out front.

French menu. Lunch, dinner, weekend brunch. Casual attire. Reservations recommended. Outdoor seating. $$

Balboa Cafe ★★☆☆☆

3199 Fillmore St., San Francisco, 415-921-3944; *www.plumpjack.com*

Situated in a historic one-story building (built in the early 1900s) in the Cow Hollow district, this American bistro has a lively lunch crowd and after-work clientele. A traditional long bar meanders along one wall of the long, narrow space, which also boasts brass rails, wood paneling, old-style hanging light fixtures, and eclectic artwork. A plush banquette and several tables sit in the space next to the front window overlooking the action on Fillmore Street, providing a comfortable spot to have a drink or wait for a table. This is a popular gathering spot for reasonably priced drinks and comfort food. Outdoor tables accommodate pooches when the weather is warm.

American menu. Lunch, dinner, Saturday-Sunday brunch. Bar. Casual attire. Valet parking. Outdoor seating. $$

Betelnut Pejiu Wu
★★☆☆☆

2030 Union St., San Francisco, 415-929-8855; *www.betelnutrestaurant.com*

Exotic drinks, a hopping bar and lounge scene, and delicious pan-Asian cuisine reel in 20- and 30-

somethings in a steady stream. The red lacquer bar, Chinese lanterns, bamboo-paneled walls and ceiling, and muted lighting set the right tone at this ever-popular Cow Hollow destination. French windows at the front of the bar and lounge open to the sidewalk to give one the feeling of dining outside. Dog-friendly tables spill onto the sidewalk in sunny weather. Betelnut Pejiu Wu (pejiu wu means "beer house") offers a large selection of beers to complement the cuisine. If you don't make reservations, prepare for a long wait.

Pan-Asian menu. Lunch, dinner. Bar. Casual attire. Reservations recommended. Outdoor seating. $$

Chaya Brasserie ★★★☆☆

132 The Embarcadero, San Francisco, 415-777-8688; *www. thechaya.com*

Chaya offers an interesting twist on two very popular cuisines—French and Japanese. Dishes include sliced roasted venison with black peppercorn sauce and purple potato purée and roasted rack of lamb with vegetable pot-au-feu and black olive tapenade. A combination of industrial and elegant décor make for sleek, sophisticated dining rooms. Orange steel beams resembling the Golden Gate Bridge and massive rectangular chandeliers add to the setting. Colorful, modern artwork and black-and-white photos adorn the walls. Located on the Embarcadero, the restaurant features floor-to-ceiling windows and outdoor tables that provide spectacular views of the bay. Diners are welcome to bring along four-legged friends to enjoy the waterfront scenery.

French, Japanese menu. Lunch, dinner. Bar. Business casual attire. Reservations recommended. Valet parking. Outdoor seating. $$$

Figaro ★★☆☆☆

414 Columbus Ave., San Francisco, 415-398-1300; *www.figaroristorante.com*

Diners will feel as though they have stepped into a ristorante in Italy when eating at Figaro, located on the main artery in North Beach. The main dining room is decorated with an elaborate ceiling mural

reminiscent of those found in Florence or Rome, and large Italian trattoria posters adorn the walls. Soft gold walls, red-tiled flooring, a small espresso bar, and Italian music enhance the scene. The lovely rear patio is tented and heated and provides a casual dining spot for pet owners. A traditional Italian menu is consistent throughout the year, but a page of specials changes each week. The self-proclaimed "house of gnocchi" also whips up a tasty tiramisu.

Italian menu. Lunch, dinner. Bar. Children's menu. Casual attire. Reservations recommended. Outdoor seating. $$

Fog City Diner ★★☆☆☆

1300 Battery St., San Francisco, 415-982-2000;
www.fogcitydiner.com

Though it's situated along the Embarcadero, Fog City Diner is more reminiscent of a train than a boat with its long interior space and chrome decor. Black-and-white tile flooring, leather retro booths, and black tables topped with crisp white linen napkins and high-quality flatware complete the setting. Both locals and tourists hunker down in the inviting booths for menu options that range from meatloaf and ribs to ethnic dishes like quesadillas and mu shu pork burritos. The raw oyster bar is also a popular draw at this unique eatery. Sidewalk seating accommodates the canine crowd.

American menu. Lunch, dinner, brunch. Bar. Children's menu. Casual attire. Outdoor seating. $$

Globe ★★☆☆☆

290 Pacific, San Francisco, 415-391-4132;
www.globerestaurant.com

An energetic Financial District destination serving American-

Italian fare, Globe stays open late, thus earning it a reputation as a favorite stop for chefs after they close their own restaurants. Two skylights add a bright, sunny glow to the restaurant's industrial decor: a zinc-topped bar and counter and exposed-brick walls with frequently changing artwork. Dogs are welcome at the streetside tables.

California, Italian menu. Lunch, dinner, late-night. Bar. Outdoor seating. $$

Paragon ★★☆☆☆

701 Second St., San Francisco, 415-537-9020;
www.paragonrestaurant.com

Just a block away from ATT Park (home of the San Francisco Giants), this brick-fronted brasserie with a glass awning serves American fare to casual business folks and an after-work drinking crowd, as well as baseball fans looking for a pre- or post-game meal. The large, contemporary space has a long bar (which serves more than 60 vodkas from all over the globe) backed by an enormous mirror. Several sidewalk tables also provide pet-friendly outdoor dining in nice weather.

American menu. Lunch, dinner. Closed Sunday. Bar. Casual attire. Reservations recommended. Outdoor seating. $$

Perry's ★☆☆☆☆

1944 Union St., San Francisco, 415-922-9022

For more than 30 years, Perry's has been a popular standby for its weekend brunch and tasty burgers, salads, and chowder.

Dogs can curl up beneath the outdoor tables on trendy Union Street where people watching is at its best, and the classic mahogany bar is perfect for a casual drink. The front and rear dining rooms, along with the atrium, feature historic one-inch octagonal tile floors, bentwood chairs, and blue and white gingham cloth-covered tables. High chalkboards with daily menus and a huge eclectic collection of memorabilia grace the walls.

American menu. Breakfast, lunch, dinner, late-night, brunch. Bar. Children's menu. Casual attire. Outdoor seating. $$

Rose Pistola ★★☆☆☆

532 Columbus Ave., San Francisco, 415-399-0499; www.rosepistolasf.com

An active entry gives way to a more sedate atmosphere at this

North Beach hot spot. Camel-colored leather banquettes and booths set off the polished wood tables, and multicolored square tiles make up the flooring. Tall front windows open to the sidewalk in front, while tables on the Stockton Street side provide a quieter setting. Outdoor heaters keep patrons and their pooches warm on cool nights. Wandering waiters serve antipasti from trays, and the exhibition kitchen showcases Italian-style cuisine with wood-fired ovens. The rustic Italian menu changes daily to reflect the freshest of locally sourced ingredients.

Italian menu. Lunch, dinner, late-night. Bar. Children's menu. Business casual attire. Reservations recommended. Valet parking. Outdoor seating. $$$

Rose's Cafe ★★☆☆☆

2298 Union St., San Francisco, 415-775-2200; www.rosescafesf.com

On the cheerful corner of Fillmore and Union Streets, Rose's Cafe serves California

and Mediterranean fare—think salads, thin-crust pizzas and grilled chicken—to a mostly local crowd. This casual off-shoot of Rose Pistola in North Beach has dog-friendly sidewalk seating protected by yellow awnings, and the inside space resembles an Italian trattoria, with multicolored floor tiles, Venetian chandeliers, mustard-colored walls, and close quarters. The brunch is extremely popular and includes a good selection of house-made Italian breads and pastries.

California, Mediterranean menu. Breakfast, lunch, dinner, brunch. Bar. Casual attire. Reservations recommended. Outdoor seating. $$

Universal Cafe ★☆☆☆☆

2814 19th St., San Francisco, 415-821-4608; *www.universalcafe.net*

While this chef-owned restaurant highlights rustic Mediterranean fare, it also has muses all over the globe, as the name suggests. Located in the Mission District near Potrero Hill, the café showcases an industrial decor, with a cement floor and marble tables, espresso bar, and counter. When the weather permits, dog owners can enjoy extra elbowroom at the outdoor tables.

California, Mediterranean menu. Dinner, brunch. Lunch, Wednesday-Friday. Closed Monday. Reservations recommended. Outdoor seating. $$

Waterfront ★★☆☆☆

Pier 7, San Francisco, 415-391-2696; *www.waterfrontsf.com*

This Embarcadero seafood restaurant incorporates its scenic views of the Bay Bridge, Treasure Island, and meandering tour boats into a romantic setting. The restaurant is split into two levels, with fine dining upstairs and a more laid-back atmosphere downstairs. On a sunny afternoon, opt for the covered terrace, but note that pooches are only welcome on the south patio under the umbrella-shielded tables.

Seafood menu. Lunch, dinner. Bar. Valet parking. Outdoor seating. $$$

Zuni Cafe ★★☆☆☆

1658 Market St., San Francisco, 415-552-2522; *www.zunicafe.com*

Celebrity chef and cookbook author Judy Rodgers continues to steer her vibrant eatery to the head of the competitive San Francisco restaurant scene. Zuni's two-story brick building on Market Street is full of light, unusual angles, and large windows. Adding to the atmosphere are the long, copper-topped bar, a large wood-burning oven, colorful modern artwork, a baby grand piano that's tickled nightly, and an array of flowers. The menu, which focuses on Mediterranean cuisine, changes daily, although the famous Caesar salad and roasted chicken are perennial favorites. Quaint sidewalk tables accommodate canines on a tree-lined strip of Market Street.

French, Italian menu. Lunch, dinner, Sunday brunch. Closed Mondays. Bar. Outdoor seating. $$$

336 rooms. High-speed Internet access. Two restaurants, bar. Fitness room, spa. Indoor pool, whirlpool. Business center. $$$$

W San Francisco ★★★☆☆

181 Third St., San Francisco, 415-777-5300, 877-946-8357; *www.whotels.com*

This hotel represents another chic spot in this national chain's list of hotels. Located in the South of Market district and adjacent to the Museum of Modern Art, the stylishly modern rooms all contain the chain's signature plush beds with luxury linens. Dogs and cats receive their own versions, complete with a nightly turndown treat, for an extra $25 and a one-time $100 cleaning fee. The eclectic and aptly named restaurant, XYZ, completes the dramatic three-story lobby.

410 rooms. High-speed Internet access. Two restaurants, two bars. Fitness room, fitness classes available, spa. Indoor pool, whirlpool. Business center. $$$

Hotel Vitale

8 Mission St., San Francisco, 415-278-3700; 888-890-8688; *www.hotelvitale.com*

Perched on the Embarcadero, this thoroughly modern and sophisticated retreat offers stunning views of the Bay Bridge, the waterfront and the busy Ferry Building Marketplace across the street. Inside the hotel, thoughtfully appointed rooms and suites impress even the most seasoned travelers. The selection of soothing music next to the CD player, plush bathrobes and slippers, rainforest showerheads and designer line of bath products give even a short visit a touch of luxury. Dogs are well cared for, too. Housekeeping provides all of the necessities—dishes, toys, towels and soft beds. Revitalize with daily complimentary yoga classes in the penthouse studio or a soak in the spa's rooftop tubs. The artfully designed Americano restaurant and lounge showcases the best offerings from the nearby farmers' market on rustic Italian and California-influenced menus.

199 rooms. High-speed, wireless Internet access. Restaurant, bar. Fitness room, fitness classes available, spa. Whirlpool. Business center.

onsite restaurant is a treat worth making time for. Pets up to 15 pounds can stay with their owners without a fee. Bowls, bottled water, and treats are complimentary, while dog walking services are available for an additional charge.

450 rooms. High-speed Internet access. Two restaurants. Fitness room, spa. Indoor pool, whirlpool. Business center. $$$

Homewood Suites Downtown Seattle
★☆☆☆☆

206 Western Ave. W., Seattle, 206-281-9393, 800-225-5466; *www.seattledowntown.homewoodsuites.com*

This downtown Seattle hotel has spacious suites featuring sleeper sofas and fully equipped kitchens with microwaves and dishwashers. The Space Needle and Seattle Center are just a short distance away. Pets up to 50 pounds are accepted on the first floor with a $200 fee; there's a limit of two dogs per room.

161 rooms. Pets accepted, some restrictions; fee. Complimentary full breakfast. Fitness room. Business center. $$

Hotel Monaco ★★★☆☆

1101 Fourth Ave., Seattle, 206-621-1770; 800-715-6513; *www.monaco-seattle.com*

This hip hotel is located near the waterfront, Pike Place Market, the Seattle Art Museum, convention centers, and shops. Rooms are contemporary and feature duvet-topped beds, L'Occitane

bath products and even all-hours yoga on the in-room TV. Pets of any size are accepted without a fee. Dog and cat treats are provided during evening turndown, and the concierge can arrange dog-sitting, walking, and spa services for your pet. The room service menu features homemade pet food.

189 rooms. High-speed, wireless Internet access. Restaurant, bar. Fitness room. Business center. $$$

Hotel Vintage Park ★★★☆☆

1100 Fifth Ave., Seattle, 206-624-8000; 800-853-3914; *www.vintagepark.com*

Built in 1922, this beautifully renovated hotel offers elegantly decorated guest rooms, each named after a local winery or vine-yard. The lobby and its fireplace are the meeting spot for nightly tastings of local wines and microbeers. Pets of any size are accepted without a fee, and are treated to food, beds, bowls, and free Vintage Park pet tags and pet T-shirts. Pets that mix and mingle at the wine hour receive grape-shaped dog treats. Dog walking and pet sitting are available for an additional charge.

126 rooms. Restaurant, bar. $$

Renaissance Seattle Hotel ★★★☆☆

515 Madison St., Seattle, 206-583-0300, 800-546-9184;
www.renaissancehotels.com

Located in downtown Seattle, this hotel combines contemporary marble and glass with earth-toned hues to convey a warm, rich ambience. Nearly everything that defines Seattle is less than a mile away—Pike Place Market and the waterfront, Pioneer Square, Safeco Field (home of the Mariners), and Seahawks Stadium. Pets of any size can stay with their owners for a $100 cleaning fee. The hotel provides loaner feeding stations, beds, salmon treats, and dog vitamin water.

553 rooms. High-speed Internet access. Two restaurants, bar. Fitness room. Indoor pool, whirlpool. Business center. $$

The Sheraton Seattle Hotel ★★★☆☆

1400 Sixth Ave., Seattle, 206-621-9000, 800-325-3535;
www.sheraton.com/seattle/

Located in downtown Seattle, this Sheraton has updated rooms with the chain's signature Sweet Sleeper Bed. The look and feel of the hotel is contemporary, from the sleek lobby to the onsite Daily Grill. Dogs weighing less than 80 pounds are welcomed with pet beds and water bowls.

840 rooms. High-speed, wireless Internet access. Restaurant, bar. Fitness room. Indoor pool. Business center. $$

Sorrento Hotel ★★★☆☆

900 Madison St., Seattle, 206-622-6400, 800-426-1265; *www.hotelsorrento.com*

Drawing on its namesake Italian village for inspiration, the Sorrento Hotel has a Mediterranean theme and superlative service. Rooms have marble baths, Egyptian cotton linens, and stereos with CD players. Pets of any size are accepted, and the hotel offers dog beds, organic treats, bowls, placemats, and poop scoopers. Dogs are allowed in Café Palma, the onsite outdoor restaurant.

76 rooms. High-speed, wireless Internet access. Restaurant, bar. Fitness room. Airport transportation available. Business center. $$$

The National Mall

www.nps.gov/nama/

This is the real Mall of America, a 309-acre national park that extends nearly two miles, from the U.S. Capitol Building on the east to the Lincoln Memorial on the west, and between Independence Avenue on the south and Constitution Avenue on the north. Must-see monuments include the Lincoln Memorial, the Jefferson Memorial, the Vietnam Memorial and of course, the Washington Monument, the 555-feet marble obelisk honoring our nation's first president. Leashed dogs are permitted on the Mall—bring plenty of pick-up bags.

Rock Creek Park

5200 Glover Rd. NE, Washington, D.C., 202-895-6070;

www.nps.gov/rocr/

Rock Creek Park offers an idyll of natural beauty in the midst of the city. The 1,754-acre park, established in 1890, is located in the northwest corner of the District. Like New York City's Central Park, Rock Creek Park has many entrances. Rock Creek, spanned by stone and iron foot bridges, winds through

the park. Wildlife abounds: Rock Creek Park has the largest concentration of raccoons in the country and is also home to red and gray foxes, as well as 200 white-tailed deer. The park is ideal for walking, hiking, jogging and biking and is open during daylight hours. Admission is free. Leashed dogs are allowed.

Chow Time

Adams Mill Bar & Grill

1813-1815 Adams Mill Road NW., Washington, D.C., 202-332-9577

Every Friday during the summer months, it's Yappy Hour from 5 p.m. to 8 p.m. at this Adams Morgan gathering place. People can enjoy half-priced appetizers (until 7 p.m.) and deals on domestic beers; pets feast on ice cream, biscuits and other treats from the nearby Doggie Style Bakery. There's no fee, but donations are occasionally accepted for local pet-related nonprofits. Yappy Hour is held on the outdoor patio year-round.

American bar-food menu. Sports-bar atmosphere. Casual dress. Lunch, dinner, late-night service.

Bangkok Bistro

3251 Prospect St. NW., Washington, D.C., 202-337-2424;

bangkokbistrodc.com

This Foggy Bottom restaurant offers the usual Thai fare (spring rolls, Pad Thai, curries) plus a wide selection of fresh fish dishes. There's an extensive martini list, and the lengthy wine list includes suggested food pairings. Pets are allowed on the outdoor patio.

Thai menu. Lunch and dinner. Casual attire.

Furin's of Georgetown

2805 M St. NW., Washington, D.C., 202-965-1000, *www.furins.com*

This Washington caterer offers light meals in a casual bakery-café setting. Choose pastries and beverages for breakfast, classic

deli sandwiches and salads for lunch and dinner. The outdoor patio is a prime spot for noshing with pets.

American menu. Breakfast, lunch, early dinner (closes at 7 p.m). Casual attire.

Papermoon

1073 31st St. NW., Washington, D.C., 202-965-6666; *www.papermoon-dc.com*

A fixture in Georgetown since 1984, Papermoon serves antipasti, pizza, pasta and salads in a relaxed setting. Three-course group menus are available for $39 and $42 per person for parties of 10 and up. Pets can join their owners on the outdoor patio, and the restaurant provides water dishes.

Italian menu. Lunch and dinner. Casual attire. Valet parking.

The Fairmont Washington, D.C. ★★★☆☆   **Lie Down**

2401 M St. NW., Washington, D.C., 202-429-2400, 800-257-7544; *www.fairmont.com*

The elegant, full-service Fairmont is an ideal base for corporate travelers or vacationers. The well-appointed rooms and suites are comfortable and spacious, and guests on the Gold Floor level are treated to additional perks, such as private check-in and dedicated concierge service. Pets are welcomed without weight limits or fees. VIDs (Very Important Dogs) are treated to hand-made treats and bottled water; collars and leashes are available to borrow. When you check in with a pet, five percent of your room charge is donated to an animal rescue organization.

415 rooms. High-speed Internet access. Two restaurants, bar. Fitness room fee, fitness classes available, spa. Business center. $$$

The Hotel George ★★★☆☆

15 E St. NW., Washington, D.C., 202-347-4200, 800-576-8331; *www.hotelgeorge.com*

Travelers book the Hotel George for its dynamic interiors and central Capitol Hill location. The dramatic rooms and suites feature bold artwork and high-tech amenities. Those traveling with pets will appreciate the hotel's "Pet Amenity Program," which includes a water and food dish, dog mat, pick-up bags, and special treats.

142 rooms. High-speed Internet access. Restaurant, bar. Fitness room. Business center. $$$

L'Enfant Plaza Hotel ★★★☆☆

480 L' Enfant Plaza SW., Washington, D.C., 202-484-1000; 800-635-5065; *www.lenfantplazahotel.com*

Rooms at the L'Enfant Plaza Hotel offer diverse views of the city. Amenities include feather-top mattresses and in-room Wi-fi (fee). A shopping complex and Metro station are located in the lower level of the building, and the hotel is steps away from the Air and Space and Holocaust museums. Up to two pets per room can join their owners with a $25 per night fee, and a $250 refundable deposit.

370 rooms. High-speed, wireless Internet access. Three restaurants, bars. Fitness room, fitness classes available. Business center. $$

The Madison ★★★☆☆

1177 15th St. NW., Washington, D.C., 202-862-1600, 866-563-9792; *www.loewshotels.com*

This hotel's beautiful Georgian architecture and clock tower cupola distinguish it from others, as does the level of hospitality provided by the friendly staff. Contemporary amenities, such as a fitness center, high-speed Internet access and an indoor pool, complement its traditional atmosphere. Traveling pets of up to 100 pounds can look forward to treats and special dishes ($35 nonrefundable room-cleaning fee). The hotel also provides a dog-walking map and information on local pet-friendly restaurants.

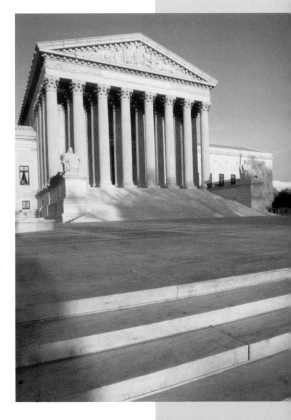

391 rooms. Restaurant, bar. Fitness room. Airport transportation available. Business center. $$$

Marriott Wardman Park Hotel ★★★☆☆

2660 Woodley Rd. NW., Washington, D.C., 202-328-2000, 888-733-3222; *www.marriotthotels.com*

This large hotel combines historic charm, beauty and convenience. A gourmet market, full-service Starbucks, jewelry store and other amenities create a home-away-from-home atmosphere. The hotel is located in the Woodley Park neighborhood near the National Zoo, and only steps from a number of distinctive restaurants. Pets up to 25 pounds are welcome; there is a $50 fee.

1,316 rooms. High-speed Internet access. Two restaurants, bar. Fitness room, spa. Business center. $$

Omni Shoreham Hotel
★★★☆☆

2500 Calvert St. NW., Washington, D.C., 202-234-0700; 888-444-6664; *www.omnihotels. com*

The sprawling Omni Shoreham combines the feel of a resort with the location of a city hotel. Take advantage of the full-service spa, or escape to nearby Rock Creek Park to hike, bike or horseback-ride. The eclectic Adams-Morgan neighborhood, with its collection of shops and ethnic restaurants, is minutes away. Pets are welcome with the payment of a $50 fee. No exotic animals (snakes are given as an example) or "extreme" animals (pit bulls are given as an example).

834 rooms. High-speed, wireless Internet access. Restaurant, bar. Fitness room, spa. Outdoor pool, whirlpool. Business center. $$$

Renaissance Mayflower Hotel ★★★☆☆

1127 Connecticut Ave. NW., Washington, D.C., 202-347-3000, 800-228-7697; *www.renaissancehotels.com*

Built in 1925 for Calvin Coolidge's inauguration, this stately, vintage high-rise property is located in the heart of the city's business district. Gilt crystal chandeliers and Oriental rugs decorate the lobby. The White House is only four blocks away. Pets under 20 pounds can stay with a $100 fee.

657 rooms. High-speed Internet access. Restaurant, bar. Fitness room. Business center. $

Sofitel Lafayette Square ★★★☆☆

806 15th N.W., Washington, D.C., 202-730-8800, 800-763-4835; *www.sofitelwashingtondc.com*

This historic hotel is located a short walk from the White House, the Metro and the National Mall. Listed on the National Register of Historic Places, it has a 1930s Art Deco theme with a contemporary edge. The lobby has a nice sitting room with

bookshelves. Four-legged friends can join their owners without fees or weight restrictions.

237 rooms. High-speed, wireless Internet access. Restaurant, bar. Fitness room. Business center. $$$

Topaz Hotel ★★☆☆☆

1733 N St. NW, Washington, D.C., 202-393-3000, 800-775-1202; *www.topazhotel.com*

Pets are as welcome as humans at this small, trendy boutique hotel with a Zen sensibility. Pet bowls and beds are available, and staff will arrange walking and grooming services for pets upon request.

99 rooms. Complimentary continental breakfast with some rates. Restaurant, bar. $$

The Westin Embassy Row ★★★☆☆

2100 Massachusetts Ave. NW., Washington, D.C., 202-293-2100;
800-937-8461; *www.westin.com*

Since 1927, this Embassy Row property has welcomed guests with turn-of-the-century style. Rooms and suites are decorated with Federal and Empire furnishings and boast beautiful views of the National Cathedral and historic Georgetown. The hotel offers dog beds and bowls and can make dog-sitting arrangements. Dogs may not be left unattended in rooms.

206 rooms. High-speed Internet access. Restaurant, bar. Fitness room. Business center. $$$

The Westin Grand ★★★☆☆

2350 M St. NW., Washington, D.C., 202-429-0100; 800-937-8461; *www.westin.com*

The Westin offers attentive service and a private, low-key environment. Rooms are comfortable and stylish with ultra-comfortable beds, sizable bathrooms, leather furniture and CD players. The hotel extends its "Heavenly Bed" promise to pets up to 40 pounds (who get their own version of the plush mattresses) and offers dog dishes and food.

263 rooms. High-speed Internet access. Two restaurants, bar. Fitness room. Outdoor pool. Airport transportation available. Business center. $$$

Willard InterContinental Washington ★★★☆☆

1401 Pennsylvania Ave. NW., Washington, D.C., 202-628-9100;
www.washington.interconti.com

Situated two blocks from the White House, this legendary Beaux Arts hotel has been at the center of Washington's political scene since 1850. This landmark's guest rooms and suites are a traditional blend of Edwardian and Victorian styles furnished in deep jewel tones. The Jenny Lind suite is perfect for honeymooners with its mansard roof and canopy bed, while the Oval suite, inspired by the office of the same name, makes guests feel like masters of the universe. Pets can weigh up to 40 pounds and must be accompanied by a $100 fee.

334 rooms. High-speed, wireless Internet access. Two restaurants, bar. Fitness room, fitness classes available, spa. Airport transportation available. Business center. $$$$

Presidential Pets

If it is indeed a dog's life, then what better place to spend it than the White House?

Legions of dogs and cats have resided at 1600 Pennsylvania Avenue during their human companions' tour as President of the United States. While most of these pets enjoyed private lives, others had their moments in the spotlight. Today's White House is home to **Barney** and **Miss Beasley**, the Bush family's Scottish terriers. A few of the pet-lebrities of recent years:

Checkers, President Richard M. Nixon's cocker spaniel, gained notoriety before either he or President Nixon set foot on the West Lawn. President Nixon gave the famous "Checkers" speech in 1952, when he was candidate for the vice-presidency: Charged with accepting illegal campaign contributions, Nixon admitted only that he accepted Checkers as a gift from a salesman.

Buddy, President William Jefferson Clinton's black Labrador retriever, became famous in the wake of the Monica Lewinsky scandal. More than once, Buddy was photographed walking alone with the President, or between the president and his wife, Hillary Rodham Clinton. Buddy shared the White House with **Socks**, First Daughter Chelsea Clinton's cat.

Yuki, President Lyndon Baines Johnson's mutt, could qualify as a presidential aide. In 1968, he helped President Johnson entertain the ambassador to Great Britain, David K.E. Bruce, by "singing" while seated in the president's lap in the Oval Office.

To learn more, check out the Presidential Pet Museum, located in Annapolis, Md., which is dedicated to the White House's four-legged residents. *www.presidentialpetmuseum.com*.

About Our Writers

Kiersten Aschauer (Atlanta) researched her chapter in this book with her beloved French bulldog Ali, who helped sniff out all the wonderful things to do, places to go and spots to shop in the city. A director at HowStuffWorks.com, she also spent six years at America Online. When not writing, you'll probably find her at Midtown's Piedmont Park with her husband, Shad, and Ali.

Lisa Bertagnoli (Washington, DC) is a freelance writer covering style, culture, restaurants, business and the arts. Her work has appeared in *Women's Wear Daily*, *Fitness*, *Self* , *Newsweek*, *Washingtonian*, and *Reader's Digest*, among others.

Lindsay Blakely (San Francisco) is a reporter at *Fortune*. She was on staff at *Business 2.0* magazine, where she regularly contributed business travel articles and blogged about new tech tools for savvy travelers. When she's not writing or traveling, she's at home in Berkeley, Calif., spoiling her zany albino cat, Minnow.

Rachel Bowie (Boston) is an editor at *Boston Common* magazine and earned her master's degree in journalism at Boston's Emerson College. Though her Beacon Hill apartment is too small for pets, she's been known to borrow the Fairmont Copley Plaza's resident labradour Catie Copley for strolls around the city.

Hillary Brylka (New York) is a freelance writer who grew up in New York City. Although her 4-year-old cat is still scheming for access to high tea at the Carlisle, and Hillary and her cohorts have moved on to chillier temperatures in Chicago, they still find city living as sweet as a walk in the park.

Juliette Guilbert (Miami, Seattle), a Seattle native, recently returned to her hometown after living in Miami. She writes about crime, politics, food, travel, kids, and architecture for *Child*, *Parenting*, *The Miami Herald*, *Florida InsideOut* and others.

Tanja Kern (San Diego) is a freelancer and former staff editor for *Better Homes and Gardens Kitchen and Bath Ideas* magazine. She has written for magazines such as *Los Angeles*, *Chicago* and *Fine Interiors*, to name a few.

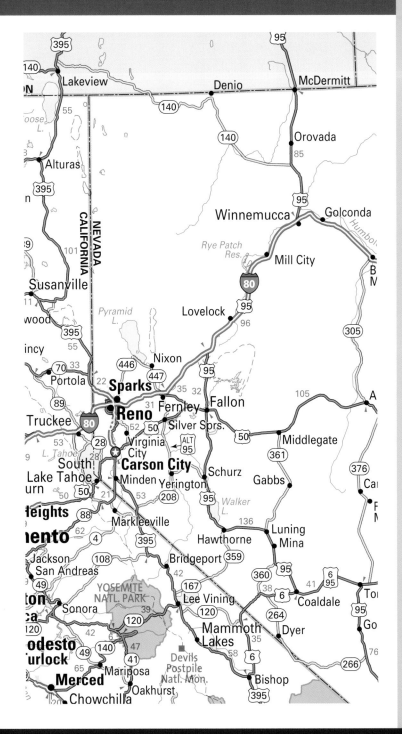

Southern California

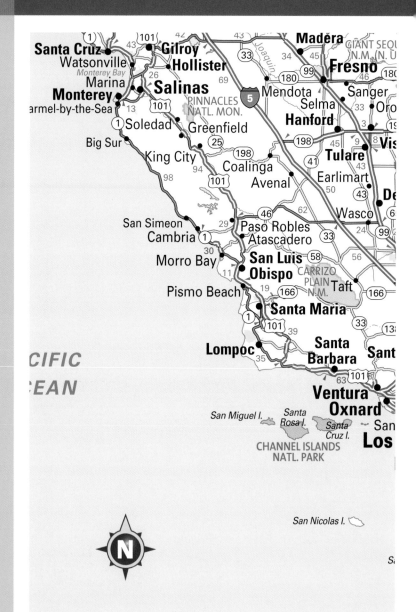

Colorado

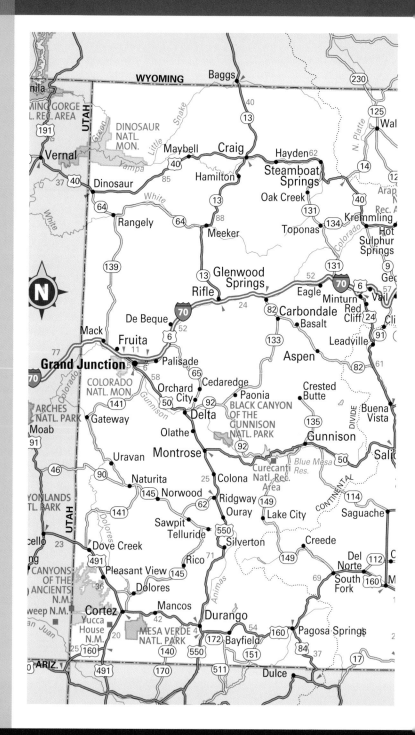

New York

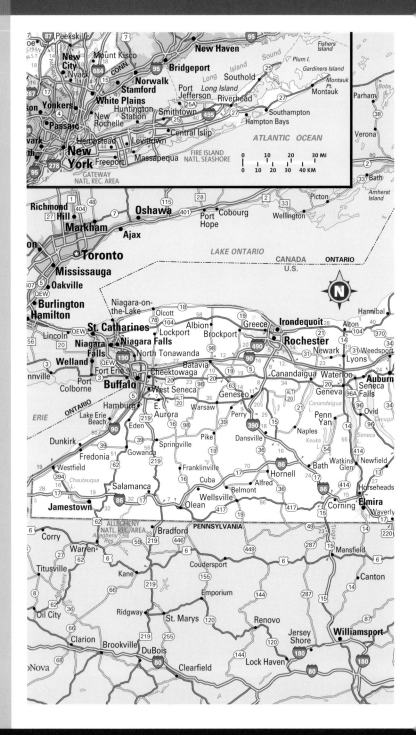

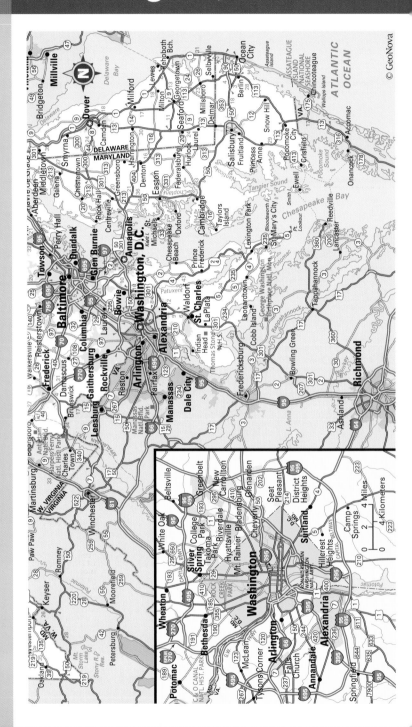

© GeoNova

Art Credits

Atlanta
1 Atlanta Skyline: "U.S. Landmarks and Travel/Getty Images:
1 Night falling on Atlanta, Georgia: "Cities of America/Getty Images
3 Dr. Martin Luther King, Jr. Historic Site statue: "U.S. Landmarks and Travel/Getty Images"
4 Bicycle And Puppy, Venice: Copyright © 2008 Corel Corp.
5 The Georgia Perspective: "U.S. Landmarks and Travel/Getty Images"
6 King Charles puppies: "2008 Jupiterimages Corporation"
7 Freeways running through Atlanta: "Cities of America/Getty Images"
8 Busy highway in Atlanta:"© Barry Howe/Corbis"

Boston
11 Quincy Market, built 1826:"Copyright © 2008 Corel Corp."
11 Statue of General George Washington: "Copyright © 2008 Corel Corp."
12 Boston Common:"Copyright © 2008 Corel Corp."
13 Green parrot:© 2008 Jupiterimages Corporation
14 John Hancock Tower: "Copyright © 2008Corel Corp."
15 Durgin Park and Market:"Copyright © 2008 Corel Corp."
16 Nine Zero Hotel:"Copyright © 2008 Nine-Zero/KimptonGroup"
17 Jack Russell Terrier with Bone: © 2008 Jupiterimages Corporation
18 Main gates to Boston Common, city landmark since 1634:"Copyright © 2008 Corel Corp."
19 Flagstaff Hill:"Copyright © 2008Corel Corp."
21 Aerial view of Boston:"© Barry Howe/Corbis"

Chicago
23 The Bowman, South Michigan Avenue: "Copyright © 2008 Corel Corp."
23 Chicago Style hotdog: © 2008 Brian Opyd, Istockphoto
24 Dog with camera: © 2008 Jupiterimages Corporation
25 Downtown Chicago with theater sign:"Cities of America/Getty Images"
26 Hotel Monaco "Copyright © 2008 HotelMonaco/KimptonGroup"
27 Buckingham Fountain in Chicago: "U.S. Landmarks and Travel/Getty Images"
29 The Bowman, South Michigan Avenue: "Copyright © 2008 Corel Corp."
30 Chicago from Lake Michigan at sunset: "© Barry Howe/Corbis"

Denver
33 RedRocks:"© Denver Metro Convention & Visitors Bureau"
33 Denver Zoo:"© Denver Metro Convention & Visitors Bureau"
34 Echo Lake:"© Denver Metro Convention & Visitors Bureau"
35 Capital Building:"© Denver Metro Convention & Visitors Bureau"
36 Rocky Mountain:"© Denver Metro Convention & Visitors Bureau"
37 Tower:"© Denver Metro Convention & Visitors Bureau"
38 Denver Skyline in the Summer:"© Denver Metro Convention & Visitors Bureau"
41 Pet Bowls at the Brown Palace:© 2008 The Brown Palace
40 Downtown View of Denver:"U.S. Landmarks and Travel/Getty Images"
42 LoDo District   "© Denver Metro Convention & Visitors Bureau"

Los Angeles
45 Kurtstejn:"© Royalty-Free/Corbis"
45 Prosciutto in Modena:"© Royalty-Free/Corbis"
46 Olvera Street Mexican Village:"Copyright © 2008 Corel Corp."
47 Olympiad 1984' sculpture in front of Stuart Ketchum YMCA:"Copyright © 2008 Corel Corp."
48 Museum of Contemporary Art at California Plaza:"Copyright © 2008 Corel Corp."

49 Brown dog looking up: © 2008 Jupiterimages Corporation
51 Clock tower, Lucerne:"© Royalty-Free/Corbis"
52 Bunker Hil view of L.A. Skyline: "Copyright © 2008 Corel Corp."
53 Jackaroo, modern sheepherder:"© Royalty-Free/Corbis"
54 Westin Bonaventure Hotel - Arco Plaza entrance: "Copyright © 2008 Corel Corp."
55 Freeway Mural of Ralph Morrison - Los Angeles Chamber Orche: "Copyright © 2008 Corel Corp."
55 Green leather dog collar: © 2008 Jupiterimages Corporation
56 4th Street cuts thru Wells Fargo Center and O'M & M Bldg.:"Copyright © 2008 Corel Corp."

Miami
59 Palm trees on beach front: "Copyright © 2008 Corel Corp."
59 Miami metro rail with city beyond, Florida: "Cities of America/Getty Images"
60 South Beach: Image provided by Greater Miami Convention & Visitors Bureau ww.gmcvb.com.
61 Boats Sailing: Image provided by Greater Miami Convention & Visitors Bureau ww.gmcvb.com.
62 Miami Buildings: Image provided by Greater Miami Convention & Visitors Bureau ww.gmcvb.com.
63 Flamingo: "© 2008 Valerie Loiseleux, Istockphoto"
64 Lincoln Road:Image provided by Greater Miami Convention & Visitors Bureau, ww.gmcvb.com.
65 Palm trees on beach front:"Copyright © 2008 Corel Corp."
66 Ocean Drive Street Sign: "U.S. Landmarks and Travel 2/Getty Images"

Minneapolis
69 Long Leash: "© 2008 Istockphoto"
69 Morning Walk by the Lake: "© 2008 Istockphoto"
71 Walking Dogs in the Snow: "© 2008 Istockphoto"
72 Relaxing Cat: © 2008 Carole Gomez, Istockphoto
73 Reflections on Mississippi River:© 2008 Geoff Kuchera, Istockphoto

Nashville
75 Road to Nashville at Dusk:"U.S. Landmarks and Travel/Getty Images"
75 Dog On the Road: "© 2008 Duncan Walker, Istockphoto"
76 Country Music Hall OF Fame: "Photo courtesy of the Tennessee Department of Tourist Development"
77 Jack's Bar-B-Que: "Copyright © 2008 Jack's Bar-B-Que"
78 Listen to the Music: © 2008 Mehmet Salih Guler, Istockphoto
79 Hermitage:"Photo courtesy of the Tennessee Department of Tourist Development"
80 Downtown Nashville:"© Wernher Krutein/Corbis"
81 Parthenon, Nashville: "Photo courtesy of the Tennessee Department of Tourist Development"
82 Kitten: © 2008 Nick Tzolov, Istockphoto
83 Bicentennial Mall: "Photo courtesy of the Tennessee Department of Tourist Development"

New York
85 Radio City Music Hall/Statue of Liberty: "U.S. Landmarks and Travel/Getty Images"
85 Central Park in winter: "Copyright © 2008 Corel Corp."
86 Dachshund dog:© 2008 Jupiterimages Corporation
87 Rockefeller Plaza and St. Patrick's:"U.S. Landmarks and Travel/Getty Images"
88 Dalmation dog : © 2008 Jupiterimages Corporation
89 View of New York City from Hoboken, New Jersey: "Cities of America/Getty Images"

Art Credits

90 Cabs in New York City:"U.S. Landmarks and Travel/Getty Images"
91 Low angle view of Brooklyn Bridge cables: "Cities of America/Getty Images"
92 Central Park in winter: "Copyright © 2008 Corel Corp."
94 Jack Russell Dog Sitting: © 2008 Jupiterimages Corporation
95 NYC cityscape (PhotoDisc):"John Kelly/PhotoDisc/Getty Images"
97 Jack Russell Fire Chief: © 2008 Stephanie Horrocks, Istockphoto
98 United Nations building: "Copyright © 2008 Corel Corp."
99 Time Warner Building "Copyright © 2008 Time Warner"
101 Dog Behing the Wheel: © 2008 Isaac Santillan, Istockphoto
102 New York City's Central Park:"© Barry Howe/Corbis"
103 The Muse Hotel: "Copyright © 2008 The Muse Hotel/KimptonGroup"
104 Dog And Owner: "Copyright © 2008 Corel Corp."
105 Landscape in autumn near Sault "Copyright © 2008 Corel Corp."

Philadelphia
107 Liberty Bell:"© 2008Anthony Sinagoga, Philadelphia Convention & Visitors Bureau"
107 Philadelphia Skyline: "© 2008 Edward Savaria, Jr., Philadelphia Convention & Visitors Bureau"
108 Penn's Landing: "© 2008 Edward Savaria, Jr., Philadelphia Convention & Visitors Bureau"
109 Valley Forge Cannon: "© 2008 Valley Forge Convention & Visitors Bureau, Philadelphia Convention & Visitors Bureau"
110 Horse of Course:© 2008Lyle Koehnlein, Istockphoto
111 Cheese steak:© 2008 Istockphoto
112 Crazy Driver:© 2008 Istockphoto
113 Philadelphia Skyline: "© 2008Anthony Sinagoga, Philadelphia Convention & Visitors Bureau"
114 FrontFacadeatDusk:"© 2008 Scott Frances, Ltd., Philadelphia Convention & Visitors Bureau"
115 StatueofBarry:"© 2008 Jim McWilliams, Philadelphia Convention & Visitors Bureau"
116 Rodin Museum: "© 2008 Edward Savaria, Jr., Philadelphia Convention & Visitors Bureau"
117 Logan Circle: "© 2008 Paul Bencivengo, Philadelphia Convention & Visitors Bureau

Portland
119 Portland, View From River Place Marina: "Copyright © 2008 Corel Corp."
119 Angelic Cat:© 2008 Mehmet Salih Guler, Istockphoto
121 Zebras: © 2008 Nick Roberts, Istockphoto
122 Downtown Portland: © 2008 Istockphoto
123 Good Friends:© 2008 Maria Bibikova, Istockphoto
124 Portland, The Japanese Gardens, Pagoda: "Copyright © 2008 Corel Corp."
125 Hotel Vintage Plaza:"Copyright © 2008 The Vintage Plaza Hotel/KimptonGroup"
126 Downtown: Copyright © 2008 Portland, Oregon Visitors Association
127 Tram overlooking Portland: "© Tim Jewett"
128 Washington Park: Copyright © 2008 Portland, Oregon Visitors Association
130 Mount Hood: Copyright © 2008 Portland, Oregon Visitors Association
131 Skybridge: Copyright © 2008 Portland, Oregon Visitors Association

San Diego
133 Cathedral in Munich:"© Royalty-Free/Corbis"
133 Sienna:"© Royalty-Free/Corbis"
134 Golden Retrievers: © 2008 Paul Erickson, Istockphoto
135 Roman sculpture:"© Royalty-Free/Corbis"
137 Mexican dancers:"© Royalty-Free/Corbis"
136 Pacific Coast Beach with foorptints:"© Royalty-Free/Corbis"
138 Hotel Solamar: "Copyright © 2008 Hotel Solamar/Kimpton Group"
139: Star of India, San Diego: "© Royalty-Free/Corbis"
140 San Diego Mission: "© Royalty-Free/Corbis"
143 Cathedral in Munich: "© Royalty-Free/Corbis"

San Francisco
145 Golden Gate Bridge: "World Commerce and Travel/Getty Images"
146 Lombard Street, San Francisco: "U.S. Landmarks and Travel/Getty Images"
147 Sea Lion Basking in the Sun: © 2008 Istockphoto
148 Fisherman's Wharf, California: "U.S. Landmarks and Travel/Getty Images"
150 Herbalist Shop - Chinatown:"Copyright © 2008 Corel Corp."
151 Grant Avenue - Chinatown: "Copyright © 2008 Corel Corp."
152 Edward Coleman House - Franklin and California Streets: "Copyright © 2008 Corel Corp."
153 Intersection of Haight-Ashbury: © 2008Robert Goldberg, Istockphoto
154 Powell Street Cable Car - Nob Hill: "Copyright © 2008 Corel Corp."
155 Manhattan skyline, including Empire State Building, sunset: "Copyright © 2008 Corel Corp."
156 Hotel Monaco: "Copyright © 2008 Hotel Monaco/KimptonGroup"
157 Dog In Sun: © 2008 Abby Wilcox, Istockphoto
158 The Thinker By Rodin - Palace Of The Legion Of Honor: "Copyright © 2008 Corel Corp."
159 San Francisco row houses at night: © Royalty-Free/Corbis
160 Golden Gate Bridge: "U.S. Landmarks and Travel 2/Getty Images"

Seattle
163 Seattle Waterfront Evening: © 2008 Istockphoto
163 Elliot Bay At Dusk: © 2008 Jo Ann Snover, Istockphoto
165 Seattle and the Mountain: © 2008 Hugo de Wolf, Istockphoto
166 Fair Grounds: © 2008 Jon Faulknor, Istockphoto
167 Farmstand: © 2008 Natalia Bratslavsky, Istockphoto
167 Canoe Dog: © 2008 Brett Lamb, Istockphoto
168 Waterview: © 2008 Jeffrey Logan, Istockphoto
169 Venice Guard Dog: © 2008 John Sigler, Istockphoto
171 Seattle Sunset: © 2008 Benjamin Goode, Istockphoto

Washington, D.C.
173 Battle of Iwo Jima/Washington Monument: "U.S. Landmarks and Travel 2/Getty Images"
173 Washington Monument: "U.S. Landmarks and Travel 2/Getty Images"
174 The White House: "World Commerce and Travel/Getty Images"
175 Take Me With You: © 2008 Josh Webb, Istockphoto
177 Column and Dome of the Jefferson Memorial: "Government and Social Issues/Getty Images"
178 Hotel George: "Copyright © 2008 Hotel George/KimptonGroup"
179 Supreme Court in Washington, DC: "World Commerce and Travel/Getty Images"
180 Battle of Iwo Jima: "U.S. Landmarks and Travel 2/Getty Images"
181 The Smithsonian Institute: "U.S. Landmarks and Travel/Getty Images"
182 Southernmost point of the continental United States: Discover Across America/Getty Images
184 Tracing heroes' names, Vietnam Memorial: "Copyright © 2008 Corel Corp."
185 Boy Walking Dog: © 2008 Ben Conlan, Istockphoto